Dedicated to curiosity and future.

What on earth is Ai?
exploring AI in the 80/20 future.

Here's a hand book on Ai. This effort is to help you understand Artificial Intelligence (AI), Generative AI, and its possibilities. This effort aims to provide a structured approach to introduce concepts in a clear and engaging manner and also provide with use cases across sectors. I have also made an attempt to capture about 20 industries and nearly 80% of today's jobs that in my opinion are most likely to get displaced within the next 10 years. Please do not treat this as scare-mongering or fear-mongering. I urge everyone to approach this very pragmatically and creatively - Perhaps the time for all of us to get trained with Pragmatic Creativity and or practice Creative pragmatism.

Author's Note

Dear Readers,

I am excited to bring this hand book on Artificial Intelligence (AI), a transformative technology that is reshaping industries, professions, and businesses worldwide. As an entrepreneur, Podcaster of Futurefast, Startup evangelist and futurist, I get called to speak to the students in Universities and colleges, Industry professionals at the industry bodies, and to start-up founders at startup ecosystems talk about how to prepare for the future. One aspect, which is likely to have the biggest impact in future is AI and herein I made an attempt to explore its vast opportunities and challenges and above all the consequences of change AI is likely to bring about in future.

In recent years, AI has emerged as a game-changer, revolutionising how we work, create, and live. Its potential to enhance efficiency, unlock new insights, and drive innovation is unparalleled. With this hand book, my aim is to bring Students, Professionals, Entrepreneurs, and Policy makers to a level of understanding of AI and the possible consequences of the change that is likely to be brought in by AI.

However, as with any transformative technology, AI also comes with its set of limitations and challenges. In this handbook, I also try to emphasise the importance of understanding these limitations, including issues of bias, privacy concerns, and ethical considerations. By shedding light on these challenges, hope to equip readers with the knowledge to navigate the AI landscape responsibly and ethically.

I have also tried to capture the areas of opportunity and also list down some of the skills if any of readers so choose to upskill themselves and explore careers in AI. This effort like everything

else is fairly comprehensive but its only getting exhaustive as you explore further.
I invite you to embark on this journey with me, exploring the world of AI from both a creative and pragmatic perspective. Whether you are an aspiring entrepreneur, a software engineer, a business leader, a policy maker or simply curious about the future of AI, I hope this handbook serves as a valuable resource.

In closing, I would like to thank Lekha Appanna, for her support and editing of this book. Despite that if you find any mistakes, they are solely mine.
I extend my sincere gratitude to the AI community, researchers, and practitioners whose groundbreaking work inspires each of us daily. I hope this handbook sparks new ideas, fosters pragmatic creativity, and ignites creative pragmatism for harnessing AI's potential for positive change.

Wishing you an enriching reading experience and an exciting future.

Warm regards,

Nanjunda Pratap Palecanda

Table of Contents

Overview 11

Core Concepts 11

Types of AI 11

- Narrow AI (Weak AI): 11
- General AI (Strong AI): 12

Applications of AI 12

Ethical and Societal Considerations 13

Future of AI 13

Importance 14

Historical Background 14

Diving deeper into Narrow AI vs. General AI 17

    Narrow AI (Weak AI) 17

        Characteristics 17

        Examples of Narrow AI 18

        Importance and Applications 18

        Limitations 19

    General AI (Strong AI) 19

        Characteristics: 19

        Challenges and Considerations: 20

    Examples of General AI (Theoretical): 20

        Importance and Potential: 20

Future Prospects: 21

    Summary 21

Types of AI Techniques and their advantages and limitations	22
1. Rule-Based Systems (Expert Systems)	22
2. Machine Learning (ML)	23
3. Deep Learning	24
4. Expert Systems with Fuzzy Logic	25
5. Natural Language Processing (NLP)	26
6. Genetic Algorithms	27
Ethical and Societal Implications	29
Bias in AI	29
Fairness in AI	30
Bias and Fairness Across Sectors and Use Cases	31
Bias and Fairness in Policy-Making	32
Privacy and Security Concerns - Present & Future	33
Mitigation Strategies	35
Generative AI	36
Core Concepts of Generative AI	37
Applications of Generative AI	39
Additional use-cases	43
How Generative AI Differs from Traditional AI	45
Possibilities and Impact of Generative AI	48
Healthcare	48
Entertainment	52
Design and Fashion	55
Ethical use of Generative AI	59

Challenges and Considerations	59
Implications of Deepfakes	61
Mitigation Strategies	62
Intellectual property (IP) and copyright	64
Challenges in IP & Copyright	64
Considerations	66
Legal and Policy Solutions	68
Future Trends	69
Generative AI research	69
Generative AI and Future Tech	73
Necessary Skills and Learnings	78
Technical Roles	79
Business Roles	80
Threats of AI	83
Threat to jobs	85
Software industry	86
Medical and Health care Community	89
Agriculture	90
Food industry	90
Law and Order	93
Armed Forces	96
Hospitality	97
Academic	97
Legal	98

Travel and Transport	99
Security	102
Construction	103
Manufacturing	104
Entertainment	105
Utilities	107
Facilities	109
Waste Management	110
Sports	112
Event management	114
Fitness	116
Preparing for Artificial Intelligence?	118
Reference materials - Books & Podcasts	125
Books	125
Podcasts	128
People who impacted and, continue to impact AI evolution and adoption.	132

Introduction to Artificial Intelligence (AI)

Artificial Intelligence, often abbreviated as AI, is a branch of computer science dedicated to creating systems and machines that can perform tasks that typically require human intelligence. The ultimate goal of AI is to develop machines that can think, reason, and problem-solve like humans, and in some cases, even surpass human capabilities.

Overview

AI encompasses a broad range of techniques, algorithms, and methodologies designed to enable machines to exhibit intelligent behaviour. It enables computers and machines to perceive, learn, reason, and take actions to achieve specific goals.

Core Concepts

- **Perception:**
  AI systems can sense and interpret the world through various sensors such as cameras, microphones, and other data sources.
- **Reasoning:**
  AI algorithms use logic and reasoning to process information, make decisions, and solve problems. This includes tasks like planning, problem-solving, and decision-making.
- **Learning:**
  One of the most crucial aspects of AI is its ability to learn from data. Machine Learning (a subset of AI) algorithms allow systems to improve their performance on tasks over time without explicit programming.

Types of AI

- **Narrow AI (Weak AI):**
  This type of AI is designed to perform a specific task or a narrow range of tasks. Examples include voice assistants like Siri or Alexa, recommendation systems on shopping websites, and spam filters in email.

- **General AI (Strong AI):**
    General AI refers to a theoretical future AI system that possesses the ability to understand, learn, and apply knowledge across a wide range of tasks. It would exhibit human-like intelligence and adaptability.

Applications of AI

AI is being integrated into various industries and domains, revolutionising how tasks are performed and problems are solved. Some common applications include:

- **Healthcare:**
    AI is used for medical imaging analysis, drug discovery, personalised medicine, and patient monitoring.
- **Finance:**
    AI algorithms are used for fraud detection, algorithmic trading, risk assessment, and customer service.
- **Transportation:**
    AI powers self-driving cars, traffic management systems, and predictive maintenance for vehicles and infrastructure.
- **E-commerce:**
    AI is used for product recommendations, personalised marketing, and chatbots for customer support.
- **Gaming:**
    AI is utilised for creating intelligent opponents, procedural content generation, and enhancing user experiences.

Ethical and Societal Considerations
As AI becomes more pervasive, there are important ethical considerations to address, such as:
- **Bias and Fairness:**
    AI systems can inherit biases from the data they are trained on, leading to discriminatory outcomes.
- **Privacy and Security:**
    AI systems often process vast amounts of personal data, raising concerns about privacy and data security.
- **Unemployment and Workforce Changes:**
    Automation driven by AI may lead to shifts in the job market, requiring new skills and training for the workforce.

Future of AI
The field of AI continues to advance rapidly, with ongoing research in areas like:
- **Deep Learning:**
    A subset of machine learning that uses neural networks with many layers to learn from vast amounts of data.
- **Natural Language Processing (NLP):**
    AI systems that can understand, generate, and respond to human language.
- **Robotics:**
    Combining AI with robotics to create intelligent machines that can interact with the physical world.

Artificial Intelligence is a transformative technology with the potential to revolutionise industries, improve efficiency, and solve complex problems. Understanding the basics of AI is crucial in today's digital age, as it shapes the future of technology and society.

Importance

Understanding the basics of AI and Generative AI is essential in today's digital age. AI is transforming industries, while Generative AI is revolutionising creativity and content creation. This knowledge equips learners with insights into cutting-edge technologies and their potential applications, paving the way for further exploration and innovation in the field.

Historical Background

Early Beginnings (1950s-1960s):
- **1950s:** The term "Artificial Intelligence" was coined by computer scientist John McCarthy at the Dartmouth Conference in 1956. The conference is considered the birthplace of AI as it brought together researchers interested in simulating aspects of human intelligence using machines.
- **Early AI Programs:** In the late 1950s and early 1960s, AI research focused on symbolic or rule-based systems. Programs like Logic Theorist (1956) by Allen Newell, J.C. Shaw, and Herbert A. Simon and the General Problem Solver (1957) by Newell and Simon demonstrated early problem-solving and reasoning capabilities.

The AI Winter (1970s-1980s):
- **Limited Progress:** In the 1970s and 1980s, progress in AI faced challenges due to limitations in computing power and the complexity of AI tasks.
- **AI Winter:** Funding for AI research decreased in the late 1970s, leading to what is known as the "AI Winter." The public and industry became disillusioned with the slow progress of AI and unmet expectations.

Rise of Expert Systems (1980s):
- **Expert Systems:** In the 1980s, AI research saw a shift towards expert systems, which were rule-based systems designed to mimic the decision-making of human experts in specific domains.
- **Applications:** Expert systems found applications in fields such as medicine, finance, and engineering. Examples include MYCIN, a system for diagnosing blood infections, and DENDRAL, a system for chemical analysis.

Neural Networks and Connectionism (1980s-1990s):
- **Connectionism:** In the late 1980s and 1990s, there was a resurgence of interest in neural networks and connectionism. Neural networks are computational models inspired by the structure and function of the human brain.
- **Backpropagation:** The development of the backpropagation algorithm for training neural networks by Geoffrey Hinton, David Rumelhart, and Ronald Williams in 1986 was a significant breakthrough.
- **Applications:** Neural networks found applications in pattern recognition, speech recognition, and other tasks.

Machine Learning and Data-Driven Approaches (1990s-2000s):
- **Machine Learning:** The 1990s and 2000s saw a shift towards machine learning and data-driven approaches within AI. Machine learning algorithms allowed systems to learn from data and make predictions or decisions without being explicitly programmed.
- **Support Vector Machines (SVMs):** SVMs, developed by Vladimir Vapnik and Corinna Cortes in the 1990s, became popular for classification tasks.

- **Big Data:** The rise of the internet and the availability of large datasets fuelled advancements in machine learning.
- **Applications:** Machine learning applications grew in areas such as spam detection, recommendation systems (e.g., Netflix, Amazon), and language processing.

Deep Learning Revolution (2010s-Present):
- **Deep Learning:** The 2010s marked a significant breakthrough with the resurgence of neural networks, particularly deep neural networks, leading to the "Deep Learning Revolution."
- **ImageNet and Convolutional Neural Networks (CNNs):** In 2012, AlexNet, a deep CNN developed by Alex Krizhevsky, Ilya Sutskever, and Geoffrey Hinton, won the ImageNet competition, demonstrating the power of deep learning for image recognition.
- **Natural Language Processing (NLP):** Deep learning has also revolutionised NLP, with models like BERT (Bidirectional Encoder Representations from Transformers) achieving remarkable results in language understanding.
- **Applications:** Deep learning has enabled breakthroughs in computer vision, speech recognition, autonomous vehicles, and many other domains.

AI Advancements and Ethical Considerations (2010s-2023):
- **AI in Industry:** AI has become more integrated into various industries, including healthcare (medical imaging, drug discovery), finance (algorithmic trading, fraud detection), and transportation (self-driving cars).
- **Ethical Considerations:** As AI becomes more prevalent, discussions on ethics, bias, transparency, and accountability have gained importance. Efforts to ensure AI is devel-

oped and used responsibly have become a significant focus.

Current State (beginning of 2024):
- **Continued Advancements:** As of early 2024, AI continues to advance rapidly. Researchers are exploring areas such as reinforcement learning, generative models (such as GANs), quantum computing for AI, and AI ethics.
- **Applications:** AI is being applied in diverse fields, from robotics and healthcare to customer service and entertainment.
- **Challenges:** Challenges remain, including ethical concerns, the need for explainable AI, data privacy, and addressing biases in AI systems.

Diving deeper into Narrow AI vs. General AI

Narrow AI (Weak AI)
Definition:
- Narrow AI, also known as Weak AI, refers to AI systems that are designed and trained for a specific task or a narrow range of tasks. These systems are focused on solving particular problems and are not capable of generalising their knowledge to other domains or tasks.

Characteristics
- **Task-Specific:** Narrow AI systems excel at specific tasks and are often optimised for performance in those areas. Examples include speech recognition, image classification, and recommendation systems.

- **Limited Scope:** They operate within a defined set of parameters and cannot perform tasks outside of their designated domain. For instance, a speech recognition AI designed for English may not work as effectively for other languages without retraining.
- **Data-Driven:** These systems rely heavily on data for training and inference. They learn patterns and make decisions based on the data they have been exposed to.

Examples of Narrow AI

- **Speech Recognition:** Systems like Siri, Alexa, and Google Assistant can understand and respond to spoken commands.
- **Image Classification:** AI models can classify images into categories such as cats or dogs, objects, or scenes.
- **Recommendation Systems:** Platforms like Netflix and Amazon use AI to recommend movies, products, or content based on user preferences and behaviour.
- **Natural Language Processing (NLP):** Chatbots and virtual assistants that can engage in conversations and provide information based on text input.

Importance and Applications

- **Efficiency:** Narrow AI systems are highly specialised, leading to increased efficiency and accuracy in specific tasks.
- **Practical Use Cases:** They find applications in industries such as healthcare (medical diagnosis), finance (algorithmic trading), and customer service (chatbots).
- **Widespread Adoption:** Narrow AI is currently the most prevalent form of AI, as it is practical and feasible for real-world deployment.

Limitations
- **Lack of Generalisation:** These systems cannot apply their knowledge to tasks beyond their specific domain.
- **Dependency on Data:** Narrow AI heavily relies on the quality and quantity of training data. Biased or limited data can lead to biased or inaccurate results.

General AI (Strong AI)
Definition:
- General AI, also known as Strong AI or Artificial General Intelligence (AGI), refers to AI systems that possess human-level intelligence and are capable of understanding, learning, reasoning, and applying knowledge across a wide range of tasks and domains.

Characteristics:
- **Human-Like Intelligence:** General AI systems would exhibit intelligence and cognitive abilities comparable to humans, including creativity, problem-solving, and adaptability.
- **Versatility:** They would not be limited to specific tasks but could apply their intelligence to various fields and scenarios.
- **Self-Learning:** These systems would be able to learn new tasks and concepts independently, without explicit programming.

Challenges and Considerations:
- **Development Challenges:** Creating General AI is a significant technical challenge due to the complexity of human intelligence.
- **Ethical and Societal Implications:** General AI raises profound ethical questions, such as ensuring safety, fairness, and control over AI systems.
- **Unpredictability:** There are concerns about the unpredictable behaviour of General AI, especially if it surpasses human intelligence.

Examples of General AI (Theoretical):
- **Human-Level Conversational Agents:** AI systems that can engage in open-ended, meaningful conversations on a wide range of topics.
- **Cognitive Robotics:** Robots with General AI could navigate complex environments, learn new tasks, and interact with humans in diverse settings.

Importance and Potential:
- **Revolutionary Impact:** General AI, if achieved, could revolutionise society, healthcare, education, and virtually every aspect of human life.
- **Autonomous Systems:** It could lead to fully autonomous vehicles, advanced healthcare diagnostics, personalised education, and scientific breakthroughs.

Future Prospects:
- **Ongoing Research:** General AI remains a long-term goal of AI research, with ongoing efforts to develop systems that approach human-level intelligence.
- **Ethical Frameworks:** Discussions around ethics, safety, and governance of General AI are essential as researchers consider its potential development.

Summary
Narrow AI:
- Specialised for specific tasks.
- Limited in scope and unable to generalise.
- Examples include speech recognition, image classification, and recommendation systems.
- Widely adopted due to practical applications.

General AI:
- Theoretical AI with human-level intelligence.
- Versatile and capable of learning across domains.
- Examples are still largely theoretical.
- Holds potential for revolutionary impact but poses significant technical and ethical challenges.
- Examples of AI in Everyday Life (e.g., recommendation systems, voice assistants)

Types of AI Techniques and their advantages and limitations

In our exploration of Artificial Intelligence (AI), it's essential to understand the diverse range of techniques that power AI systems. These techniques form the foundation of how machines perceive, learn, reason, and make decisions. Let's dive into the different types of AI techniques:

1. Rule-Based Systems (Expert Systems)

Description:
Rule-based systems, also known as expert systems, are one of the earliest forms of AI techniques. They operate based on predefined rules and logic.

Characteristics:
Knowledge Base: Expert systems have a knowledge base containing rules and facts about a specific domain.
Inference Engine: The inference engine applies rules to the knowledge base to draw conclusions or make decisions.
Example: A medical diagnosis system where rules define symptoms and corresponding diseases.

Advantages:
Interpretability: Rules are easy to interpret and understand, making them transparent.
Explicit Knowledge Representation: Knowledge is explicitly encoded in rules, allowing for easy modification and reasoning.

Limitations:
 Limited Flexibility: Rule-based systems are rigid and struggle with complex, uncertain, or evolving environments.
 Maintenance Overhead: As rules increase, maintenance becomes challenging and time-consuming.

2. Machine Learning (ML)

Description:
 Machine Learning is a subset of AI where algorithms enable machines to learn from data and improve over time without explicit programming.

Types of Machine Learning:
 Supervised Learning: Algorithms learn from labeled data, making predictions or classifications based on input-output pairs.
 Unsupervised Learning: Algorithms identify patterns and relationships in unlabelled data.
 Reinforcement Learning: Agents learn to make decisions by interacting with an environment, receiving rewards or penalties.

Applications:
 Classification: Identifying spam emails, recognising handwritten digits.
 Regression: Predicting house prices, stock prices.
 Clustering: Customer segmentation, grouping similar items.

Advantages:
 Flexibility: ML models can adapt to new data and learn patterns without explicit programming.

Complex Pattern Recognition: Capable of handling complex relationships in data.
Automation: Once trained, ML models can make predictions or decisions autonomously.

Limitations:
Data Dependency: ML models require large amounts of labeled data for training, which can be costly and time-consuming.
Black Box: Deep learning models, in particular, can be hard to interpret, leading to a lack of transparency.
Overfitting: ML models can memorise noise in the training data, leading to poor generalisation on unseen data.

3. Deep Learning

Description:
Deep Learning is a subset of Machine Learning that uses neural networks with many layers to learn from large amounts of data.

Key Concepts:
Neural Networks: Modelled after the human brain, with layers of interconnected nodes (neurons).
Convolutional Neural Networks (CNNs): Specialised for processing grid-like data, such as images and videos.
Recurrent Neural Networks (RNNs): Effective for sequence data, like time series or text.

Applications:
Computer Vision: Image and video recognition, object detection.
Natural Language Processing (NLP): Speech recognition, language translation, sentiment analysis.

Advantages:
- **Hierarchical Feature Learning:** Deep learning models automatically learn hierarchical representations of data.
- **State-of-the-Art Performance:** Achieves impressive results in computer vision, speech recognition, and NLP.
- **Feature Extraction:** Deep neural networks can extract features from raw data, reducing the need for manual feature engineering.

Limitations:
- **Computational Complexity:** Training deep networks can be computationally intensive, requiring powerful hardware.
- **Data Dependency:** Like other ML techniques, deep learning models require large amounts of labeled data.
- **Interpretability:** Deep learning models are often considered black boxes, making it challenging to understand how they arrive at decisions.

4. Expert Systems with Fuzzy Logic

Description:
Fuzzy Logic extends traditional Boolean logic to handle uncertainty and imprecision.

Characteristics:
- **Fuzzy Sets:** Elements have degrees of membership (e.g., "very hot" instead of just "hot").
- **Fuzzy Rules:** Rules can express vague relationships (e.g., "if it's somewhat cold, then increase the heater slightly").

Applications:
> **Control Systems:** Air conditioning, washing machines.
> **Pattern Recognition:** Handwriting recognition, image processing.

Advantages:
> **Handling Uncertainty:** Fuzzy logic allows for handling uncertain or imprecise data more effectively.
> **Expressiveness:** Rules in fuzzy logic can express relationships in a more nuanced manner.
> **Fault Tolerance:** Fuzzy logic systems can tolerate imprecise inputs and still produce reasonable outputs.

Limitations:
> **Complexity:** Designing fuzzy logic systems with many rules can become complex.
> **Knowledge Acquisition:** Developing the initial set of fuzzy rules requires domain expertise.
> **Computational Overhead:** Fuzzy logic computations can be more resource-intensive compared to traditional logic.

5. Natural Language Processing (NLP)

Description:
> Natural Language Processing focuses on enabling computers to understand, interpret, and generate human language.

Techniques:
> **Text Preprocessing:** Tokenisation, stemming, and lemmatizations.
> **Named Entity Recognition (NER):** Identifying entities like names, organisations, and locations.

Sentiment Analysis: Determining the sentiment (positive, negative, neutral) in text.

Applications:
Chatbots and Virtual Assistants: Customer service, information retrieval.
Language Translation: Google Translate, language learning apps.
Text Summarisation: Condensing large texts into concise summaries.

Advantages:
Human-Computer Interaction: Enables machines to understand and generate human language, facilitating communication.
Wide Range of Applications: NLP is used in chatbots, language translation, sentiment analysis, and more.
Information Extraction: Can extract structured information from unstructured text data.

Limitations:
Ambiguity: Natural language is inherently ambiguous, leading to challenges in interpretation.
Context Understanding: NLP models may struggle with understanding context, sarcasm, or humour.
Language Dependency: Models trained on one language may not generalise well to others.

6. Genetic Algorithms
Description:
Genetic Algorithms are inspired by the process of natural selection and evolution.

Key Concepts:
    Population: A set of candidate solutions.
    Selection: Choosing individuals from the population for reproduction.
    Mutation and Crossover: Introducing variation and combining traits from selected individuals.

Applications:
    Optimisation Problems: Traveling salesman problem, scheduling.

Advantages:
    Global Optimisation: Genetic algorithms are suitable for finding global optima in complex search spaces.
    Parallelism: Can be parallelised, allowing for faster optimisation in some cases.
    No Derivative Requirements: Unlike some optimisation techniques, genetic algorithms do not require derivatives of the objective function.

Limitations:
    Convergence Speed: Genetic algorithms can be slow to converge, especially for large and complex problems.
    Difficulty in Parameter Tuning: Finding appropriate genetic algorithm parameters can be challenging.
    Limited Applicability: Not suitable for all optimisation problems, particularly those with well-defined constraints.

Summary:
    Rule-Based Systems: Transparent and interpretable, but limited in flexibility and scalability.

Machine Learning: Flexible and powerful for complex pattern recognition, but data-dependent and can be black boxes.

Deep Learning: Excels in hierarchical feature learning and state-of-the-art performance but can be computationally intensive and lack interpretability.

Expert Systems with Fuzzy Logic: Effective for handling uncertainty and nuanced relationships, but can be complex to design.

Natural Language Processing (NLP): Enables human-computer interaction and a wide range of applications, but faces challenges with ambiguity and context.

Genetic Algorithms: Suitable for global optimisation in complex search spaces, but may be slow to converge and require careful parameter tuning.

Ethical and Societal Implications

Bias in AI
Definition:
Bias in AI refers to systematic and unfair discrimination or favouritism toward certain groups, individuals, or outcomes in the data or algorithms used by AI systems.

Sources of Bias:
Data Bias: When training data is unrepresentative or skewed, leading to biased models.
Algorithmic Bias: Bias introduced during the design or implementation of algorithms, such as biased features or incorrect assumptions.
Historical Bias: Reflecting societal biases present in historical data, perpetuating existing inequalities.

Examples of Bias:
> **Gender Bias:** AI systems in recruitment might favour male candidates due to historical hiring patterns.
> **Racial Bias:** Facial recognition systems may have higher error rates for certain ethnicities.
> **Socioeconomic Bias:** Loan approval algorithms might discriminate against low-income applicants.

Fairness in AI
Definition:
> Fairness in AI aims to ensure that AI systems treat all individuals and groups fairly and without discrimination, regardless of their characteristics.

Types of Fairness:
> **Individual Fairness:** Similar individuals should receive similar outcomes.
> **Group Fairness:**
>> **Demographic Parity:** Equal representation of groups in outcomes.
>> **Equality of Opportunity:** Equal chances for success regardless of group membership.
>
> **Algorithmic Fairness:**
>> **Preventing Discrimination:** Ensuring no protected attributes (like race or gender) are used for decision-making.
>> **Counterfactual Fairness:** Ensuring similar outcomes for similar individuals.

Examples of Fairness:
   Fair Hiring Practices: AI tools in recruitment should ensure equal consideration for all applicants, regardless of demographic factors.
   Loan Approval: Fairness in loan approval algorithms means offering loans based on creditworthiness rather than demographics.

Bias and Fairness Across Sectors and Use Cases
Healthcare:
   Bias: Diagnostic AI tools may have biases based on historical patient data, leading to misdiagnoses for certain groups.
   Fairness: Ensuring equal access to healthcare recommendations and treatments for all patients.

Criminal Justice:
   Bias: Predictive policing algorithms may over-police certain neighbourhoods, perpetuating racial biases.
   Fairness: Ensuring fair and unbiased risk assessments for individuals in the criminal justice system.

Finance:
   Bias: Loan approval algorithms may discriminate against minority or low-income applicants.
   Fairness: Offering loans based on creditworthiness and financial history rather than demographic factors.

Hiring and Human Resources:
   Bias: AI-based recruitment tools may favor certain demographics, leading to biased hiring practices.

Fairness: Implementing blind recruitment processes to prevent bias based on gender, race, or other factors.

Bias and Fairness in Policy-Making
Challenges:

Algorithm Transparency: Ensuring policymakers understand the AI systems they use and their potential biases.

Data Governance: Establishing data collection and handling protocols to prevent biased data inputs.

Ethical Guidelines: Developing ethical guidelines for the use of AI in policy-making to promote fairness and accountability.

Solutions:

Algorithm Auditing: Regular audits of AI systems to detect and mitigate biases.

Diverse Representation: Including diverse voices and perspectives in policy-making to address biases.

Education and Awareness: Training policymakers on AI ethics and fairness principles.

Conclusion:
Addressing bias and promoting fairness in AI applications across sectors and policy-making is crucial for building trust, avoiding discrimination, and ensuring equitable outcomes. By understanding the sources of bias, types of fairness, and implementing appropriate measures, we can work towards developing AI systems that serve all individuals and communities fairly and ethically.

Continued research, collaboration between stakeholders, and the development of robust policies and guidelines are essential steps toward achieving bias-free and fair AI applications in various sectors and policy-making.

Privacy and Security Concerns - Present & Future

Privacy and security concerns arising from AI are significant considerations in the present and are expected to become even more critical in the future. Let's explore these

Present Concerns
1. Data Privacy:
Data Collection: AI systems often require vast amounts of data for training, raising concerns about how personal data is collected, stored, and used.

Sensitive Information: AI may inadvertently access and process sensitive personal information, such as health records or financial data.

2. Biometric Data:
Facial Recognition: The use of facial recognition technology raises privacy concerns regarding surveillance and the potential for misuse.

Voice Recognition: Voice-based AI assistants can collect and store voice recordings, raising questions about privacy and consent.

3. Cybersecurity:
Vulnerabilities: AI systems can be vulnerable to cyber attacks, including adversarial attacks that manipulate AI models.

Data Breaches: The large datasets used in AI applications can become targets for hackers, leading to data breaches and privacy violations.

4. Algorithmic Bias:

Discriminatory Outcomes: Biased algorithms can lead to discriminatory outcomes, impacting privacy rights and exacerbating societal inequalities.

Lack of Transparency: Opacity in AI decision-making processes can make it difficult to identify and correct biased algorithms.

Future Concerns
1. Deepfake Technology:

Manipulated Media: Deepfake technology can create highly realistic fake videos, audio, and images, raising concerns about misinformation and privacy violations.

Impersonation: Individuals could be impersonated using deepfake technology, leading to privacy breaches and reputational harm.

2. Autonomous Systems:

Privacy Invasion: Autonomous vehicles and drones equipped with AI may inadvertently invade privacy by capturing and processing personal data in public spaces.

Surveillance: AI-powered surveillance systems could track individuals' movements and behaviours, raising concerns about mass surveillance.

3. Internet of Things (IoT):

Data Collection: AI-driven IoT devices, such as smart home assistants, collect vast amounts of personal data, raising privacy concerns.

Security Risks: Vulnerabilities in IoT devices could lead to unauthorised access to personal information and cyber attacks.

4. Privacy-Preserving AI:
Preserving Privacy: As AI systems become more sophisticated, there is a need for techniques that allow AI to operate on sensitive data without exposing it.

Federated Learning: Privacy-preserving methods like federated learning enable AI models to be trained across decentralised data sources without sharing raw data.

Mitigation Strategies
1. Data Minimisation:
Limit Data Collection: Collect only necessary data and minimise the retention of sensitive information.

2. Privacy by Design:
Embed Privacy: Integrate privacy features into AI systems from the design phase to ensure privacy considerations are fundamental.

3. Transparency and Explainability:
Interpretability: Make AI systems more transparent and explainable to users and regulators to understand how decisions are made.

4. Regulation and Compliance:
GDPR, CCPA: Compliance with regulations such as the General Data Protection Regulation (GDPR) and California Consumer Privacy Act (CCPA) to protect user privacy.

5. Ethical Frameworks:
Ethical Guidelines: Develop and adhere to ethical frameworks for AI development and deployment to ensure fairness, accountability, and respect for privacy.

6. Cybersecurity Measures:
   Secure Development: Implement robust cybersecurity measures to protect AI systems from cyber threats and vulnerabilities.

7. User Awareness and Consent:
   Informed Consent: Ensure users are informed about how their data will be used and obtain explicit consent for data processing.

Conclusion:
As AI technologies continue to advance, addressing privacy and security concerns is crucial to building trust and ensuring responsible AI deployment. Current and future challenges, such as data privacy, algorithmic bias, deepfake technology, and IoT vulnerabilities, require proactive measures.

By implementing data minimisation, privacy by design, transparency, compliance with regulations, ethical frameworks, cybersecurity measures, and user awareness, we can mitigate the risks associated with AI. Collaboration between stakeholders, including policymakers, industry, researchers, and users, is essential to navigate these complex privacy and security challenges effectively.

Generative AI

Generative AI is a subset of artificial intelligence (AI) focused on the creation of new content, such as images, text, audio, and videos, that is not based on existing examples. It involves using algorithms to generate original and often realistic content that can be used in various applications, including art, design, music, and more. Generative AI has gained significant attention in recent years for its ability to produce creative and novel outputs.

Core Concepts of Generative AI

1. Generative Models:
Definition: Generative models are AI algorithms designed to learn the underlying patterns and characteristics of a dataset to generate new, realistic samples.

Examples: Variational Autoencoders (VAEs), Generative Adversarial Networks (GANs), and Autoregressive Models.

2. GANs (Generative Adversarial Networks):
Overview: GANs consist of two neural networks, the generator and the discriminator, trained simultaneously in a competitive manner.

Generator: Creates new data samples from random noise.

Discriminator: Distinguishes between real and generated data.

Training: The generator aims to fool the discriminator into accepting its generated samples as real, while the discriminator aims to correctly identify fake samples.

3. VAEs (Variational Autoencoders):
Overview: VAEs are generative models that learn a latent representation of data and generate new samples by sampling from this learned distribution.

Encoder: Maps input data to a latent space.

Decoder: Reconstructs data from the latent space.

Variational Inference: VAEs use variational inference to approximate the true data distribution and generate new samples.

4. Autoregressive Models:

Overview: Autoregressive models predict the next element in a sequence based on previous elements.

Sequential Generation: Generates sequences (text, audio, etc.) one element at a time, conditioning on previous elements.

Example: Language models like GPT-3 (Generative Pretrained Transformer 3) use autoregressive methods to generate human-like text.

5. Reinforcement Learning for Generative AI:

Overview: Reinforcement learning can be used in generative AI to learn policies for generating sequences or images.

Reward Signals: The model receives rewards based on the quality or realism of generated outputs.

Example: Reinforcement learning can be used to train an AI artist to create visually appealing artwork.

6. Creative Applications:

Art and Design: Generative AI is used to create unique art pieces, designs, and visual effects.

Music Generation: AI can compose original music and generate new musical compositions.

Text Generation: Natural language models can produce human-like text, stories, and poems.

Image Synthesis: AI can generate photorealistic images, create new faces, and alter images.

7. Ethical Considerations:

Bias and Fairness: Generative models can inherit biases from training data, leading to biased outputs.

Misuse and Deepfakes: Concerns about the misuse of generative AI for creating deepfakes or spreading misinformation.

Ownership and Copyright: Questions arise about the ownership and copyright of AI-generated content.

8. Challenges:

Training Complexity: Generative models can be computationally intensive and require large datasets.

Mode Collapse: GANs may suffer from mode collapse, where the generator produces limited diversity in generated samples.

Evaluation: Assessing the quality and realism of generated outputs is challenging.

Applications of Generative AI

Art and Creativity: Generating art, design, and visual effects.

Content Creation: Creating text, stories, poems, and articles.

Image Synthesis: Generating photorealistic images, faces, and scenes.

Music Composition: Composing original music and generating new melodies.

Data Augmentation: Generating synthetic data for training machine learning models.

Fashion Design: Creating new fashion designs and styles.

Some of these companies are at the forefront of utilising AI for art, creativity, content creation, image synthesis, music composition, data augmentation, and fashion design. Their platforms and tools empower users to leverage AI technologies for various creative and practical applications.

Art and Creativity:
  RunwayML:
    Services: Offers tools for artists and creators to use AI in their creative projects.
    Features: Enables style transfer, generating art with GANs, and creating interactive experiences.
    Website: https://runwayml.com/
  DeepArt.io:
    Services: Provides AI-powered tools for transforming photos into artwork.
    Features: Offers style transfer, AI painting, and customised art generation.
    Website: https://deepart.io/

Content Creation:
  OpenAI (GPT-3):
    Services: Offers the GPT-3 (Generative Pre-trained Transformer 3) language model for content generation.
    Features: Capable of generating human-like text for articles, stories, and more.
    Website: https://www.openai.com/gpt-3/
  Writesonic:
    Services: AI-powered writing assistant for content creation.
    Features: Generates marketing copy, blog posts, social media content, and more.
    Website: https://writesonic.com/

Image Synthesis:
  NVIDIA AI Art Gallery:

Services: Showcases AI-generated art created with GANs.

Features: Offers a gallery of AI-generated images and allows users to explore and interact with AI art.

Website: https://www.nvidia.com/en-us/ai-art-gallery/

Artbreeder:

Services: Platform for creating and exploring AI-generated images.

Features: Users can blend and evolve images, create portraits, landscapes, and more.

Website: https://www.artbreeder.com/

Music Composition:

Amper Music:

Services: AI music composer for creating custom music tracks.

Features: Users can input parameters like mood, style, and tempo to generate unique compositions.

Website: https://www.ampermusic.com/

AIVA:

Services: AI music composer for composers and musicians.

Features: Generates classical music, film scores, and other genres based on user input.

Website: https://www.aiva.ai/

Data Augmentation:

Augmenter:

Services: Python library for image augmentation using AI techniques.

Features: Allows users to create augmented datasets for machine learning tasks.
Website: https://augmentor.readthedocs.io/en/master/

Synthetic Data (from H2O.ai):
Services: Offers synthetic data generation for machine learning.
Features: Helps create diverse and realistic datasets for training AI models.
Website: H2O.ai Synthetic Data https://www.H2O.ai/SyntheticData

Fashion Design:
Replika Software:
Services: AI-powered fashion design software.
Features: Enables virtual design and prototyping, trend analysis, and customisation.
Website: https://www.replikasoftware.com/

IBM Watson Fashion Advisor:
Services: AI-driven fashion recommendation and styling.
Features: Provides personalised fashion suggestions based on user preferences and trends.
Website: IBM Watson Fashion Advisor

Generative AI opens up a world of creative possibilities and has the potential to revolutionise various industries. However, it also raises ethical considerations regarding bias, misuse, ownership, and the societal impact of AI-generated content. As the field continues to evolve, understanding its core concepts and applications is essential for those interested in exploring the frontier of AI creativity.

Additional use-cases
Apart from enabling various sectors and sector leaders, AI has been a game-changer for startups, enabling them to compete with established enterprises by leveraging innovative technologies. Here are a few real-world examples of how AI is helping startups grow and become formidable players in their industries:

1. **Casetext**: Casetext is a legal research platform that uses AI to make legal research more efficient and accessible. Their AI-powered tool, CARA (Case Analysis Research Assistant), helps lawyers find relevant cases and statutes quickly and accurately. This AI technology has allowed Casetext to compete with larger legal research companies by offering a cost-effective and efficient solution. Until they built the ai capability, they were one of the digital options but not the 'ONE' with that differentiator which lead them to get acquired by Thomson Reuters for $650 million in 2023.
2. **UiPath**: UiPath has become a leading player in the field of robotic process automation (RPA). Their AI-powered RPA platform automates repetitive tasks in businesses, such as data entry and processing, freeing up employees to focus on more strategic work. UiPath's innovative use of AI has helped them compete with established players and attract clients from various industries. Today, post IPO it is counted among the most influential AI companies and has acquired multiple ai startups.
3. **ZestFinance**: ZestFinance is a fintech startup that uses AI to improve credit underwriting processes. Their AI platform analyses thousands of data points to assess creditworthiness, allowing lenders to make more accurate lending decisions. This has enabled ZestFinance to compete with tra-

ditional credit scoring agencies and offer a more inclusive and fair approach to credit assessment.
4. **Gong**: Gong is a startup that provides an AI-driven sales analytics platform. Their AI analyzes sales conversations and provides insights to help sales teams improve their performance. By leveraging AI, Gong has been able to compete with larger sales analytics companies and attract clients from Fortune 500 companies. Gong is competing against the biggest of Business Intelligence companies today.
5. **DataRobot**: DataRobot is a startup that offers an automated machine learning platform. Their AI platform helps businesses build and deploy machine learning models quickly and efficiently, without requiring deep technical expertise. This has enabled startups and small businesses to leverage AI for data-driven decision-making, competing with larger enterprises that have dedicated data science teams.
6. **Grammarly**: Grammarly is a startup that has disrupted the writing assistance industry with its AI-powered grammar checker. Their AI technology analyses text for grammar, punctuation, style, and tone, offering real-time suggestions to improve writing. This has allowed Grammarly to compete with established writing tools and attract millions of users worldwide.
7. **Scale AI**: Scale AI is a startup that provides AI-powered data labelling services for machine learning projects. Their platform helps companies annotate and label large datasets quickly and accurately, which is essential for training AI models. Scale AI's technology has enabled startups to accelerate their AI projects and compete with larger companies in deploying AI-driven solutions.

These examples demonstrate how startups are using AI to innovate, automate processes, improve decision-making, and deliver valuable solutions to customers. Its important note among them that most of these startups started of with the technologies reliable and prevalent then (as most of them have been around for a long time). It is be leveraging AI technologies, these startups could level the playing field and compete with established enterprises in various industries and even get ahead of the competition.

How Generative AI Differs from Traditional AI

Generative AI differs from traditional AI in several key ways, primarily in its focus on creating new content rather than performing specific tasks or making predictions based on existing data. Let's explore the differences between Generative AI and Traditional AI:

Traditional AI:
1. Task-Specific:
    Focus: Traditional AI, also known as Narrow AI or Weak AI, is designed for specific tasks and applications.
    Examples: Speech recognition, image classification, recommendation systems, and chatbots are typical examples of traditional AI applications.

2. Data-Driven Learning:
    Training: Traditional AI systems are trained on large datasets to recognise patterns and make predictions.
    Supervised Learning: Many traditional AI models use supervised learning, where labeled data is provided to teach the model.

3. Problem-Solving Approach:

Rule-Based Systems: Traditional AI often relies on rule-based systems or algorithms with explicit instructions on how to solve a problem.

Decision Trees: Algorithms like decision trees and support vector machines are commonly used for classification tasks.

4. Predictive and Reactive:

Predictive: Traditional AI systems are designed to predict outcomes based on historical data.

Reactive: They react to inputs based on predefined rules or patterns, without the ability to generate new content.

5. Examples:

Spam Detection: Traditional AI can be used to detect spam emails by learning patterns in email content.

Image Recognition: Identifying objects in images based on trained patterns is another traditional AI application.

Generative AI:
1. Content Creation:

Focus: Generative AI, on the other hand, is focused on creating new content that is not based on existing examples.

Novelty: It aims to generate new images, text, audio, and more, often in a creative and realistic manner.

2. Generative Models:

Variety: Generative AI uses models like Generative Adversarial Networks (GANs), Variational Auto-encoders (VAEs), and autoregressive models to create diverse outputs.

Learning Distributions: These models learn the underlying distribution of data and generate new samples from this learned distribution.

3. Creative Approach:
Originality: Generative AI is more about creativity and imagination, producing outputs that do not exist in the training data.
Artistic Expression: It is used in art, music, design, and other creative fields to generate new and innovative content.

4. Unsupervised and Reinforcement Learning:
Unsupervised Learning: Generative AI often uses unsupervised learning techniques to learn from unlabelled data and find patterns.
Reinforcement Learning: Some generative models incorporate reinforcement learning to improve output quality over time.

5. Examples:
Art Generation: Creating new artworks, designs, and visual effects using generative AI.
Text Generation: Writing stories, poems, and articles with AI-generated content.
Music Composition: Generating original music and melodies using AI.

Differences in Application:
Traditional AI: Used for solving specific tasks efficiently, such as classification, prediction, and automation of repetitive tasks.

Generative AI: Used for creating new content, fostering creativity, and exploring novel possibilities in art, design, music, and other creative domains.

Summary:
Traditional AI:
- Task-specific applications.
- Data-driven learning for prediction and classification tasks.
- Reactive and rule-based systems.
- Examples include spam detection, image recognition, and chatbots.

Generative AI:
- Focuses on creating new content and generating novel outputs.
- Uses generative models like GANs and VAEs.
- Creative and imaginative approach.
- Examples include art generation, text generation, and music composition.

Generative AI marks a departure from the traditional task-specific approach of AI, offering exciting opportunities for creativity and innovation. It enables machines to not only perform tasks but also to create and imagine, pushing the boundaries of what AI can achieve in artistic and creative fields.

Possibilities and Impact of Generative AI
Healthcare

Generative AI holds significant promise for transforming various aspects of the healthcare industry. Here are several ways Generative AI is poised to help businesses and industries in the healthcare space:

Medical Imaging and Diagnostics

Generative AI can enhance medical imaging in several ways:
- **Image Enhancement:** Algorithms can improve the quality of medical images, making it easier for doctors to spot anomalies.
- **Image Generation**: AI can generate synthetic images to augment datasets, which can be especially useful in training deep learning models for tasks like tumour detection.
- **Segmentation:** Precisely identifying and segmenting organs or tissues in medical images is crucial for diagnosis and treatment planning. Generative models can assist in this segmentation process.

Drug Discovery and Development
- **Molecule Generation:** Generative models can assist in creating novel molecular structures with desired properties, aiding in drug discovery.
- **Virtual Screening**: AI models can virtually screen vast libraries of compounds to predict their potential efficacy and safety, speeding up the drug development process.
- **Side Effect Prediction:** Predicting potential side effects of drugs before clinical trials can save time and resources.

Personalised Medicine
- **Patient Data Analysis:** Generative AI can analyse vast amounts of patient data, including genomics, lifestyle factors, and medical history, to create personalised treatment plans.

Outcome Prediction: Predicting patient outcomes based on individual characteristics can help doctors tailor treatments.

Precision Medicine: By understanding genetic variations and their implications on treatment response, AI can aid in precision medicine approaches.

Electronic Health Records (EHR) Management

Data Entry and Coding: Generative AI can help automate data entry tasks, reducing the burden on healthcare staff.

Natural Language Processing (NLP): NLP models can extract valuable information from unstructured EHR data, improving diagnoses and treatment planning.

Anomaly Detection: AI can flag anomalies in patient records, such as potential errors or inconsistencies.

Telemedicine and Remote Monitoring

Virtual Assistants: AI-powered virtual assistants can improve patient interactions, answer questions, and schedule appointments.

Remote Monitoring: AI can analyse data from wearables and IoT devices, providing real-time insights into patient health.

Decision Support: During remote consultations, AI can provide decision support for healthcare providers based on the patient's data.

Operational Efficiency

Resource Optimisation: AI can optimise hospital workflows, such as scheduling operating rooms or predicting patient admissions, leading to better resource allocation.

Supply Chain Management: Predicting demand for medical supplies and medications can prevent shortages and reduce costs.

Fraud Detection: Detecting fraudulent claims or activities in healthcare billing using AI algorithms.

Mental Health

Chatbots and Virtual Therapists: AI-driven chatbots can provide mental health support, offering resources and interventions.

Sentiment Analysis: Analysing social media and patient data for sentiment can provide insights into mental health trends and needs.

Early Detection: AI can help in early detection of mental health conditions by analysing speech patterns or online behaviour.

Research and Clinical Trials

Literature Review: AI can sift through vast amounts of research literature to provide insights and identify potential areas of study.

Patient Recruitment: AI can match eligible patients to clinical trials more efficiently, speeding up the research process.

Drug Repurposing: Identifying existing drugs that can be repurposed for new treatments using AI models.

In conclusion, Generative AI has the potential to revolutionise healthcare by improving diagnostics, accelerating drug discovery, personalising treatment plans, enhancing patient care, and optimising operational efficiency. However, challenges such as data privacy, model interpretability, and regulatory hurdles must be addressed to fully realise these benefits.

Entertainment

Generative AI is already making significant impacts in the entertainment industry, offering new tools for content creation, personalisation, and audience engagement. Here's how Generative AI is helping businesses and industries in the entertainment space:

Content Creation
    Art Generation: Generative models can create original artworks, illustrations, and designs for various purposes, from video game assets to movie concept art.
    Music Composition: AI can compose original music tracks in various genres, catering to specific moods or scenes for films, games, or advertisements.
    Scriptwriting: AI can assist in generating scripts for movies, TV shows, or advertisements, providing creative prompts or even full drafts.

Visual Effects and Animation
    Animation Assistance: Generative AI can help in creating animations, reducing manual labor in tasks like keyframing and tweening.
    Enhanced Visual Effects: AI can generate realistic and detailed visual effects for movies, TV shows, and games, such as lifelike CGI characters or environments.
    Face and Character Generation: AI-driven tools can create realistic human faces and characters, streamlining character design and animation processes.

Video Editing and Post-Production
    Automated Editing: AI can analyse footage and automatically generate edits based on style, pacing, and storytelling conventions.

Image and Video Enhancement: Enhancing video quality, removing noise, or upscaling resolution using AI algorithms.

Deepfakes: While controversial, Generative AI can create convincing deepfake videos, used in entertainment for special effects or digital doubles.

Gaming

Procedural Content Generation: AI can generate game levels, environments, and assets procedurally, reducing development time and adding variety.

NPC Behaviour: AI can create non-player characters (NPCs) with more realistic behaviours, enhancing gameplay experiences.

Dialogue Generation: AI can generate dynamic and context-aware dialogues for NPCs, improving storytelling in games.

Virtual Production

Virtual Sets: Generative AI can create virtual sets and backgrounds for film and TV production, reducing the need for physical sets.

Real-time Rendering: AI-powered real-time rendering engines can create high-quality visuals on the fly, enabling virtual production techniques.

Virtual Actors: AI-driven characters and avatars can interact with live actors in real-time, blending virtual and physical performances.

Personalisation and Recommendation

Content Recommendation: AI algorithms can analyse user preferences and viewing habits to recommend personalised content on streaming platforms.

Interactive Storytelling: AI-powered interactive narratives, where the audience can influence the story's direction, creating personalised experiences.

Ad Personalisation: AI can tailor advertisements based on user data, improving relevance and engagement.

Augmented Reality (AR) and Virtual Reality (VR)

AR Filters and Effects: AI can create interactive AR filters for social media platforms, allowing users to augment their reality.

VR Environments: AI can generate immersive VR environments for gaming, training simulations, or virtual tours.

Motion Capture: AI-driven motion capture technology can create realistic character animations for VR experiences.

Localisation and Translation

Subtitles and Dubbing: AI can automate subtitle generation and dubbing processes, making content accessible to global audiences.

Content Translation: Translating content into multiple languages using AI-powered language models, expanding reach and accessibility.

Cultural Adaptation: AI can analyse cultural nuances and adapt content accordingly for different markets or regions.

Story Generation

Narrative Design: AI can assist writers and creators in developing storylines, character arcs, and plot twists.

Dynamic Storytelling: Using AI, stories can dynamically adapt based on user interactions or preferences, creating personalised narratives.

Fan Fiction and Fan Art: AI models can generate fan art and stories based on popular franchises or characters, engaging fan communities.

Copyright and Content Protection

Content Filtering: AI algorithms can help platforms detect and remove copyrighted content, ensuring compliance and protection.

Watermarking: Generative AI can embed invisible watermarks into content, aiding in tracking and protecting intellectual property.

In summary, Generative AI is revolutionising the entertainment industry by offering new avenues for content creation, personalisation, efficiency, and audience engagement. As these technologies continue to evolve, they will likely become even more integrated into various aspects of entertainment, from filmmaking to gaming to digital media consumption.

Design and Fashion

Generative AI is making a significant impact on the design and fashion industries, offering innovative tools for creativity, customisation, and efficiency. Here's how Generative AI is helping businesses and industries in the design and fashion space:

Fashion Design

Design Inspiration: Generative models can generate endless design variations, providing designers with inspiration for new collections.

Pattern Generation: AI can create intricate and unique patterns for fabrics, helping designers develop one-of-a-kind textiles.

Colour Palette Creation: AI algorithms can suggest colour palettes based on trends, seasons, or brand identity.

Fabric and Material Design

Material Synthesis: Generative AI can simulate and generate virtual fabrics and materials, allowing designers to visualise and experiment with textures.

Textile Design: AI can assist in designing textiles with specific properties like stretch, durability, or breathability.

Material Optimisation: Using AI to optimise material usage, reducing waste in the production process.

Customisation and Personalisation

Custom Clothing: Generative AI enables made-to-measure clothing by creating patterns tailored to individual body measurements.

Personalised Recommendations: AI algorithms can analyse customer preferences and suggest personalised designs or product combinations.

Virtual Try-On: AI-powered virtual fitting rooms allow customers to see how clothing looks on them without physically trying it on.

Rapid Prototyping and Iteration

3D Modelling: AI can generate 3D models of fashion designs, aiding in rapid prototyping and visualisation.

Virtual Sampling: Using AI, designers can create virtual samples of garments, reducing the need for physical prototypes.

Iterative Design: AI tools allow for quick iteration on designs, enabling designers to explore numerous variations efficiently.

Trend Forecasting and Analysis
> **Trend Prediction:** AI can analyse social media, runway shows, and online searches to predict upcoming fashion trends.
> **Consumer Insights:** Generative AI helps in understanding consumer preferences and behaviours through data analysis.
> **Market Demand Prediction:** Using AI algorithms to forecast demand for specific styles or products, optimising production and inventory management.

Sustainable Fashion
> **Material Recycling:** AI can help in developing recycled materials for fashion, promoting sustainability.
> **Waste Reduction:** Generative AI can optimise garment production processes to minimise waste.
> **Circular Economy:** AI-driven platforms can facilitate clothing rental or resale markets, extending the lifecycle of garments.

Virtual Fashion Shows and Retail
> **Virtual Runway:** AI enables the creation of virtual fashion shows and presentations, reducing the need for physical events.
> **Virtual Retail Spaces:** AI can design virtual stores and showrooms, enhancing the online shopping experience.
> **AR/VR Try-On:** Using augmented reality (AR) or virtual reality (VR), customers can virtually try on clothing and accessories before purchasing.

Branding and Marketing
> **Visual Identity:** Generative AI can assist in creating logos, branding materials, and visual elements for fashion brands.

Content Generation: AI-powered tools can generate social media content, such as images, videos, and captions, tailored for fashion brands.

Influencer Matching: AI algorithms can match brands with suitable influencers based on audience demographics and brand image.

Supply Chain Optimisation

Predictive Analytics: AI can forecast demand and optimise production schedules, reducing overstocking and underproduction.

Supplier Matching: AI-driven platforms can help connect fashion brands with sustainable and ethical suppliers.

Quality Control: Using AI for automated quality control in manufacturing processes, ensuring consistency and efficiency.

Collaborations and Co-Creation

Designer Collaboration: AI can facilitate collaborations between designers, artists, and brands, fostering creativity and innovation.

Customer Co-Creation: Platforms powered by AI enable customers to co-create designs, allowing for unique and personalised products.

Cross-Industry Innovation: AI-driven design tools can be used across industries, such as architecture or automotive, for cross-disciplinary inspiration.

In summary, Generative AI is revolutionising the design and fashion industries by offering new possibilities for creativity, sustainability, customisation, and efficiency. As these technologies continue to evolve, they will likely become indispensable tools for designers, brands, and consumers alike, shaping the future of fashion and design.

Ethical use of Generative AI

The ethical use of Generative AI, particularly in the context of deepfakes, presents several challenges and considerations that need to be addressed. Here are some key points:

Challenges and Considerations

Misinformation and Fake Content:
Deepfakes created using Generative AI can be used to spread misinformation, fake news, or defamatory content.
Without proper safeguards, it can be challenging to distinguish between real and manipulated content.

Privacy Concerns:
Generative AI raises significant privacy concerns, especially when used to create fake videos or images of individuals without their consent.
Privacy laws and regulations may struggle to keep pace with the rapid advancements in AI technology.

Reputation Damage:
Deepfakes can be used maliciously to damage the reputation of individuals, organisations, or public figures.
Once a deepfake is circulated widely, it can be challenging to control its spread and mitigate the damage.

Consent and Rights:
> The use of Generative AI to create deepfakes raises questions about consent and the rights of individuals featured in the content.
> Clear guidelines and ethical frameworks are needed to ensure that deepfakes are not created or distributed without consent.

Bias and Fairness:
> AI models used in Generative AI can inherit biases from the training data, leading to biased or discriminatory outcomes.
> Ensuring fairness and mitigating bias in deepfake creation is essential to prevent harm to marginalised groups.

Security Risks:
> Malicious actors can use Generative AI to create convincing phishing scams, voice impersonations, or other forms of cyberattacks.
> Enhanced security measures are needed to detect and prevent these types of attacks.

Legal and Regulatory Gaps:
> Current legal frameworks may not adequately address the challenges posed by deepfakes and Generative AI.
> Policymakers and regulators are working to develop guidelines and regulations to address these issues.

Implications of Deepfakes

Political Manipulation:
Deepfakes can be used to create fake videos of political figures, leading to political manipulation and destabilisation.
Elections and public discourse can be negatively impacted by the spread of false information.

Financial Fraud:
Deepfakes can be used for financial fraud, such as creating fake videos of executives to trick employees into transferring funds.
Businesses and individuals are at risk of falling victim to these types of scams.

Cyberbullying and Harassment:
Deepfakes can be used for cyberbullying and harassment, creating harmful content targeted at individuals.
Victims of deepfake attacks can suffer emotional distress and reputational harm.

Legal and Reputational Consequences:
The proliferation of deepfakes can lead to legal battles and challenges in proving the authenticity of content.
Organisations may face reputational damage if they are associated with the creation or dissemination of deepfakes.

Impact on Journalism:
>Deepfakes pose challenges for journalism and media credibility, as it becomes harder to verify the authenticity of visual content.
>Journalists and media organisations need to develop new tools and practices to verify the legitimacy of videos and images.

Mitigation Strategies

Technological Solutions:
>Developing AI algorithms that can detect and identify deepfakes.
>Implementing watermarking or cryptographic methods to verify the authenticity of content.

Education and Awareness:
>Educating the public about the existence and potential dangers of deepfakes.
>Training individuals to recognise signs of manipulation in videos and images.

Ethical Guidelines:
>Establishing clear ethical guidelines for the creation and use of Generative AI, particularly in creating deepfakes.
>Ensuring transparency about the use of AI in content creation and dissemination.

Legal Frameworks:
>Enacting laws and regulations that specifically address the creation, distribution, and use of deepfakes.

Holding platforms accountable for hosting or promoting harmful deepfake content.

Collaboration:
Collaboration between technology companies, policymakers, researchers, and civil society to develop effective solutions.
Sharing best practices and lessons learned in combating deepfakes.

User Authentication:
Implementing robust authentication methods for verifying the identity of individuals in videos and images.
Encouraging users to adopt two-factor authentication and other security measures to prevent impersonation.

Media Literacy:
Promoting media literacy programs to help individuals critically evaluate online content.
Teaching skills to discern between genuine and manipulated media.

In conclusion, the ethical use of Generative AI, especially in the context of deepfakes, requires a multifaceted approach that involves technological advancements, education, legal frameworks, and collaboration among various stakeholders. By addressing these challenges and considerations, it is possible to mitigate the negative impacts of deepfakes while harnessing the benefits of Generative AI for positive applications.

Intellectual property (IP) and copyright

Generative AI poses several challenges and considerations related to intellectual property (IP) and copyright, primarily due to its ability to create content that may blur the lines of ownership and originality. Here are some key points to consider:

Challenges in IP & Copyright

Ownership of Generated Content:
Generative AI can create new artworks, music, designs, and texts, raising questions about who owns the rights to these creations.

It becomes challenging to determine whether the AI creator, the user providing input, or the owner of the AI model holds the rights.

Derivative Works and Fair Use:
Generative AI may generate content that is considered a derivative work based on existing copyrighted material.

Determining what constitutes fair use of copyrighted material in AI-generated works can be complex and subjective.

Licensing and Permissions:
Users of Generative AI may not always consider or obtain the necessary licenses or permissions for the data used to train the AI models.

Lack of proper licensing and permissions can lead to infringement issues when AI-generated works are used or distributed.

Plagiarism and Replication:
    Generative AI can replicate styles, patterns, and characteristics of existing works, potentially leading to accusations of plagiarism.
    Identifying instances where AI-generated content crosses the line from inspiration to infringement can be challenging.

Attribution and Authorship:
    AI-generated content may lack clear attribution or authorship, making it difficult to credit the original creators or identify responsible parties.
    Establishing provenance and ownership of AI-generated works can be murky without clear guidelines.

International Copyright Laws:
    Copyright laws vary across countries, adding complexity when AI-generated content is distributed globally.
    Harmonising international copyright laws to address AI-generated works is a significant challenge.

Reverse Engineering and Data Privacy:
    Reverse engineering AI models to reproduce or modify AI-generated works may raise IP and privacy concerns.
    Protecting the proprietary nature of AI models and the data used to train them is crucial.

Considerations
Clear Policies and Guidelines:
Establishing clear policies and guidelines for the creation, ownership, and use of AI-generated content.

Clarifying who holds the rights to AI-generated works and under what circumstances they can be used.

Copyright Registration:
Encouraging creators to register AI-generated works with copyright offices to establish legal protection and ownership.

Addressing challenges related to registering works created by AI rather than human authors.

Transparency and Disclosure:
Ensuring transparency in disclosing when AI was used to create content, especially in commercial or public settings.

Clearly indicating AI-generated works to avoid misleading audiences about authorship.

Licensing Models:
Developing new licensing models tailored to AI-generated content, such as AI-generated music or art libraries.

Exploring options for licensing AI models themselves for creative use.

Digital Watermarking and Tracking:
    Implementing digital watermarking or tracking mechanisms to embed ownership information into AI-generated content.
    Facilitating the tracking of ownership and usage rights across digital platforms.

Ethical Use and Attribution:
    Promoting ethical use of Generative AI and adherence to copyright laws and fair use principles.
    Encouraging proper attribution even in AI-generated works to respect the contributions of original creators.

Collaboration and Standards:
    Collaborating with industry stakeholders, legal experts, and policymakers to develop standardised practices for handling AI-generated content.
    Establishing industry-wide standards for licensing, attribution, and ownership of AI-generated works.

Educating Creators and Users:
    Providing education and training to creators and users of Generative AI about IP laws, fair use, and ethical considerations.
    Empowering creators to understand their rights and responsibilities when using AI tools.

Legal and Policy Solutions

Updates to Copyright Laws:
Considering updates to copyright laws to address the unique challenges posed by AI-generated content.
Clarifying definitions of authorship, ownership, and derivative works in the context of AI.

AI-Specific Regulations:
Introducing AI-specific regulations or guidelines that outline responsibilities and rights related to AI-generated content.
Addressing liability issues when AI is used to create infringing works.

Data Protection Laws:
Strengthening data protection laws to safeguard the privacy of individuals whose data is used to train AI models.
Balancing IP rights with data privacy considerations when training AI models on user-generated content.

International Collaboration:
Encouraging international collaboration and harmonisation of laws to create consistent frameworks for AI-generated content.
Participating in international treaties and agreements to address cross-border copyright issues.

In conclusion, the rise of Generative AI presents complex challenges for intellectual property and copyright, particularly in determining ownership, attribution, and fair use of AI-generated content. Addressing these challenges requires a multi-faceted approach involving legal updates, clear guidelines, technological solutions, and collaboration among stakeholders to ensure responsible and ethical use of Generative AI while protecting the rights of creators and original content owners.

Future Trends

Generative AI research is a rapidly evolving field with numerous exciting trends and advancements on the horizon. Here are some future trends and areas of advancement in

Generative AI research

1. Improved Realism in Generated Content:
Advancements in Generative Adversarial Networks (GANs) and other models will lead to even more realistic and high-fidelity generated images, videos, and audio.
Techniques like StyleGAN and BigGAN have already shown impressive results, and future models will continue to push the boundaries of realism.

2. Enhanced Control and Manipulation:
Researchers are working on methods to provide users with more control over the generated content, such as specifying attributes like age, gender, pose, and emotions.
Techniques like disentangled representation learning aim to separate different factors of variation in data, allowing for more precise manipulation.

3. Multimodal Generative Models:

Future Generative AI models will be able to generate content across multiple modalities simultaneously, such as generating images from textual descriptions or vice versa.

This includes advancements in text-to-image synthesis, speech-to-image, and image-to-speech synthesis.

4. Continual Learning and Lifelong AI:

Research is focusing on developing Generative AI models that can learn continually from new data without catastrophic forgetting.

Lifelong learning approaches will enable AI systems to accumulate knowledge and skills over time, adapting to new tasks and environments.

5. Generative Models for Science and Healthcare:

There's a growing interest in using Generative AI for scientific discovery, such as generating new molecules for drug discovery, protein folding prediction, and materials design.

In healthcare, Generative AI will continue to advance personalised medicine by creating patient-specific models and treatments.

6. Cross-Domain Applications:

Generative AI models trained on data from one domain can be applied to other domains, known as domain adaptation.

This enables applications like transferring styles across domains (e.g., artistic style transfer for images), domain translation (e.g., translating sketches to realistic images), and more.

7. Ethical and Responsible AI:

Research efforts will focus on developing AI models that are more transparent, fair, and less biased.

Explainability techniques for Generative AI will become crucial to understand and trust the decisions made by these models.

8. Zero-shot and Few-shot Learning:

Zero-shot learning aims to teach AI models to perform tasks with no training examples, relying on transfer learning and generalisation.

Few-shot learning techniques allow AI models to learn from a few examples, enabling rapid adaptation to new tasks.

9. Energy Efficiency and Model Compression:

As Generative AI models become larger and more complex, research will focus on making them more energy-efficient and computationally lightweight.

Techniques like model pruning, quantisation, and distillation will be employed to reduce the size and memory footprint of models.

10. Privacy-Preserving Generative Models:

With increasing concerns about data privacy, Generative AI research will focus on developing methods to generate data while preserving individual privacy.

Federated learning, differential privacy, and encrypted computation techniques will be explored for privacy-preserving Generative AI.

11. Interactive and Co-Creative Systems:

Future Generative AI systems will enable interactive collaboration between humans and AI, allowing for co-creation of art, music, stories, and designs.

Real-time feedback loops will enable artists, designers, and creators to guide and influence the generative process.

12. Adversarial Robustness:
Research will focus on developing Generative AI models that are robust against adversarial attacks, where small perturbations can lead to incorrect outputs.
Adversarial training and defence mechanisms will be explored to improve the security of Generative AI systems.

13. Unsupervised and Self-Supervised Learning:
Advancements in unsupervised learning will enable Generative AI models to learn from unlabelled data, reducing the need for large annotated datasets.
Self-supervised learning approaches will also gain traction, where AI learns from the data itself, creating its own supervision signals.

14. Hardware Acceleration and Specialised Architectures:
With the increasing computational demands of Generative AI models, there will be a focus on developing specialised hardware accelerators and architectures.
GPUs, TPUs, and neuromorphic chips will continue to evolve to support the training and inference of large-scale Generative AI models.

15. Robotic and Embodied AI:
Generative AI will play a role in creating more lifelike and responsive robotic systems, enabling robots to generate realistic movements, expressions, and behaviours.
Embodied AI research will focus on integrating Generative AI with physical robotic systems for applications in healthcare, manufacturing, and more.

In conclusion, the future of Generative AI research holds immense potential for advancements in realism, control, multimodal capabilities, continual learning, cross-domain applications, ethics, and more. These trends will shape the development of AI systems that are not only more intelligent and creative but also more responsible, efficient, and adaptable to various tasks and environments.

Generative AI and Future Tech

Generative AI has the potential to be integrated with various other technologies, leading to innovative applications and advancements across different fields. Here are some ways

Generative AI could be integrated with other technologies:

1. Generative AI and Robotics:

Robotic Movement Generation: Generative AI can be used to generate realistic and adaptive movements for robots, improving their agility and responsiveness.

Behavioural Synthesis: AI models can create diverse and natural behaviours for robots, enabling them to interact more effectively with humans and their environment.

Robotics Design: AI can assist in designing robot components and structures, optimising for strength, weight, and functionality through generative design.

2. Generative AI and IoT (Internet of Things):

Smart Environments: AI-generated content can be used to create immersive and context-aware experiences in IoT-connected environments.

Anomaly Detection: AI models can generate normal behaviour patterns in IoT data, helping to detect anomalies and potential issues.

Predictive Maintenance: Using Generative AI, predictive models can be developed for IoT devices to forecast maintenance needs and prevent failures.

3. Generative AI and Blockchain:

Authenticity Verification: AI-generated content can be stored on a blockchain to verify its authenticity and provenance.

Smart Contracts: Blockchain-based smart contracts can automate transactions related to AI-generated content, such as licensing and royalties.

IP Protection: Blockchain can be used to protect the intellectual property of AI-generated works, providing a transparent and immutable record of ownership.

4. Generative AI and Augmented Reality (AR)/Virtual Reality (VR):

Immersive Experiences: Generative AI can create realistic and interactive environments for AR/VR applications, enhancing immersion.

Virtual Characters and Avatars: AI-generated characters and avatars in AR/VR can exhibit more lifelike behaviours and expressions.

Real-time Content Generation: AI can dynamically generate content in AR/VR environments based on user interactions, creating personalised experiences.

5. Generative AI and 3D Printing:

Design Optimisation: AI-generated designs can be optimised for 3D printing, reducing material usage and printing **time.**

Customisation: 3D printed objects can be customised using AI-generated patterns, textures, and shapes.

Prototyping: AI can generate 3D models for rapid prototyping, enabling quick iteration and testing of designs.

6. Generative AI and Biotechnology:

Drug Discovery: AI-generated molecules and compounds can be used in drug discovery and development, speeding up the process.

Protein Design: AI can assist in designing new proteins with desired properties for medical and industrial applications.

Genomic Data Analysis: AI models can analyse and interpret genomic data, aiding in personalised medicine and genetic research.

7. Generative AI and Marketing/Advertising:

Personalised Content: AI-generated content can be tailored to individual preferences and behaviours for targeted marketing campaigns.

Virtual Try-On: In fashion and retail, AI can generate virtual try-on experiences, allowing customers to preview products before purchase.

Ad Creative: AI can assist in creating compelling and visually appealing ad creatives, optimising for engagement and conversion rates.

8. Generative AI and Finance:

Trading Strategies: AI-generated models can analyse market data to develop trading strategies and predictions.

Risk Assessment: AI can generate synthetic data for risk assessment and stress testing in finance and insurance industries.

Fraud Detection: Generative AI can help in detecting fraudulent activities by generating scenarios and anomalies for analysis.

9. Generative AI and Healthcare:

Medical Imaging: AI-generated images can assist in training medical imaging models for better diagnosis and treatment planning.

Patient Data Synthesis: AI can generate synthetic patient data to augment real datasets for training healthcare AI models.

Robot-Assisted Surgery: In robotic surgery, AI can generate surgical plans and simulations for precision and safety.

10. Generative AI and Gaming:

Procedural Content Generation: AI can generate game levels, environments, and assets on-the-fly for dynamic and infinite gameplay.

NPC Behaviour: AI-generated behaviours and dialogues for non-player characters (NPCs) can enhance realism and immersion in games.

Dynamic Storytelling: Games can use Generative AI to create branching narratives and personalised storylines based on player choices.

11. Generative AI and Agriculture:
Crop Management: AI-generated models can analyse agricultural data to optimise crop yields, pest management, and irrigation.
Plant Breeding: AI can assist in developing new plant varieties with desirable traits through generative design.
Farm Robotics: AI can generate control strategies for robotic systems used in agriculture, such as autonomous tractors and drones.

12. Generative AI and Education:
Personalised Learning: AI-generated content can provide personalised learning materials tailored to individual student needs and learning styles.
Language Learning: AI can create language learning materials, such as exercises, dialogues, and pronunciation guides.
Simulated Environments: Generative AI can create virtual learning environments and simulations for hands-on training and education.

13. Generative AI and Transportation:
Autonomous Vehicles: AI-generated models can simulate various driving scenarios for training autonomous vehicle systems.
Traffic Simulation: AI can generate realistic traffic flow simulations for urban planning and optimisation.
Vehicle Design: AI-generated designs can optimise vehicle aerodynamics, reducing fuel consumption and emissions.

14. Generative AI and Supply Chain Management:
   Demand Forecasting: AI can generate demand forecasts for products, optimising inventory management and supply chain logistics.
   Supply Chain Visualisation: AI-generated visualisations can provide insights into supply chain operations, identifying bottlenecks and inefficiencies.
   Predictive Maintenance: AI-generated models can predict equipment failures and maintenance needs in supply chain operations.

15. Generative AI and Energy:
   Energy Optimisation: AI can generate optimal energy usage patterns for buildings, factories, and smart grids.
   Renewable Energy: AI-generated models can predict renewable energy generation from sources like solar and wind for better integration into the grid.
   Smart Grid Management: AI can optimise grid operations and distribution using generative models for load forecasting and balancing.

These are just a few examples of how Generative AI can be integrated with various technologies to create innovative solutions and applications across industries. As Generative AI continues to evolve, its integration with other technologies will likely lead to even more transformative advancements and novel use cases.

Necessary Skills and Learnings

Whether in technical or business roles, there are essential skills and learnings one should acquire to effectively use AI in their professions. These skills encompass both technical understanding and broader business acumen. Here's a breakdown of skills for both technical and business roles:

Technical Roles

Programming Languages:
Python: Widely used in AI development for libraries like TensorFlow, PyTorch, and scikit-learn.
R: Especially useful for statistical analysis and data visualisation.

Machine Learning and Deep Learning:
Understanding of fundamental machine learning concepts like regression, classification, clustering, and neural networks.
Knowledge of deep learning frameworks such as TensorFlow, PyTorch, and Keras.
Ability to implement and train machine learning models, and understand hyperparameter tuning.

Data Science and Data Engineering:
Proficiency in data manipulation and analysis using libraries like Pandas, NumPy, and SciPy.
Skills in data preprocessing, cleaning, and feature engineering.
Understanding of databases and SQL for data extraction and manipulation.

AI Development:
Knowledge of AI development methodologies, including Agile and DevOps practices.
Ability to design, develop, and deploy AI models into production environments.
Familiarity with model deployment tools and platforms like Docker and Kubernetes.

Natural Language Processing (NLP):
Understanding of NLP concepts for tasks like sentiment analysis, named entity recognition, and text classification.
Knowledge of NLP libraries such as NLTK, SpaCy, and Transformers.

Computer Vision:
Understanding of computer vision algorithms for tasks like object detection, image classification, and image segmentation.
Proficiency in OpenCV and deep learning frameworks for computer vision tasks.

Big Data Technologies:
Familiarity with big data technologies such as Apache Hadoop, Spark, and Kafka for handling large-scale data.
Ability to work with distributed computing and parallel processing.

Model Evaluation and Interpretation:
Skills in model evaluation metrics like accuracy, precision, recall, F1-score, ROC curves, etc.
Understanding of model explainability techniques like SHAP values, LIME, and feature importance.

Business Roles

AI Literacy and Understanding:
Familiarity with AI concepts, terminologies, and its potential applications in various industries.

Understanding of how AI can drive business value, improve processes, and enhance decision-making.

Data Literacy:
Ability to understand and interpret data, including basic statistical concepts.
Knowledge of data sources, data quality, and data governance practices.

Domain Knowledge:
Deep understanding of the industry or domain in which AI will be applied.
Knowledge of industry-specific challenges, trends, and opportunities.

Strategic Thinking:
Ability to identify business problems or opportunities where AI can be leveraged effectively.
Strategic planning skills to develop AI initiatives aligned with organisational goals.

Data-driven Decision Making:
Understanding of how AI insights can influence decision-making processes.
Ability to interpret AI-generated analytics and reports for business impact.

Project Management:
Skills in project planning, execution, and monitoring.
Ability to lead AI projects, manage resources, and ensure timely delivery.

Ethical and Regulatory Awareness:
- Understanding of ethical considerations in AI, including bias, privacy, and transparency.
- Knowledge of AI regulations and compliance requirements in relevant industries.

Communication and Collaboration:
- Strong communication skills to articulate AI concepts and findings to stakeholders.
- Collaboration skills to work effectively with cross-functional teams, including data scientists, engineers, and business leaders.

Change Management:
- Ability to drive organisational change to integrate AI solutions into existing workflows.
- Skills in training and up-skilling teams to embrace AI technologies.

Additional Considerations:

Continuous Learning: AI is a rapidly evolving field, so a commitment to ongoing learning and staying updated with the latest advancements is crucial.

Networking: Engage with AI communities, attend conferences, and participate in online forums to learn from others and stay connected with industry trends.

Hands-on Experience: Whether through personal projects, hackathons, or work assignments, practical experience is invaluable for applying AI knowledge in real-world scenarios.

Industry Certifications: Consider relevant certifications such as Google TensorFlow Developer Certificate, Microsoft Certified: Azure AI Engineer Associate, or AWS Certified Machine Learning – Specialty.

Combining technical skills with business acumen is increasingly essential for professionals in both technical and business roles to leverage AI effectively. Understanding AI's capabilities, limitations, and ethical considerations is crucial for making informed decisions and driving successful AI initiatives within organisations. Continuous learning, hands-on experience, and collaboration across teams will be key to success in integrating AI into various professions.

World has already seen Minister for AI and Chief AI officer. Opportunity is only as much as one can imagine it to be. The skills mentioned above are only indicative and current. One needs to actively start thinking the possibilities.

Threats of AI

Many prominent figures in the tech industry, including Elon Musk have been highlighting several potential threats and concerns related to Artificial Intelligence (AI). Here are some of the common threats of AI as frequently highlighted:
- **Job Displacement**: One of the most widely discussed concerns is the potential for AI and automation to replace human jobs. As AI systems become more advanced, they could automate tasks across various industries, leading to job loss for certain sectors of the workforce.
- **Autonomous Weapons**: Elon Musk, among others, has expressed concerns about the development of autonomous weapons powered by AI. These weapons could

make deadly decisions without human intervention, raising ethical questions and the potential for misuse.
- **AI Bias and Discrimination**: AI systems are only as good as the data they are trained on. If the training data is biased, AI systems can perpetuate or even amplify existing biases and discrimination in areas such as hiring, admissions (to schools & Colleges, clubs and associations), lending, and law enforcement.
- **Loss of Control**: There are concerns about the possibility of AI systems becoming too autonomous and making decisions that humans cannot understand or control. This "black box" problem raises questions about accountability and oversight.
- **Privacy and Surveillance**: The proliferation of AI-powered surveillance systems raises privacy concerns. AI can be used to analyse vast amounts of data, including personal information, leading to concerns about surveillance and data misuse.
- **Existential Risks**: Elon Musk has notably expressed concerns about the long-term risks of super intelligent AI. He has warned about the potential for AI to surpass human intelligence and act in ways that could be harmful to humanity, posing existential risks.
- **Ethical Dilemmas**: As AI becomes more sophisticated, it raises complex ethical questions. For example, how should autonomous vehicles make split-second decisions in life-or-death situations? Who is responsible when an AI system makes a mistake?
- **Economic Inequality**: While AI has the potential to create wealth and innovation, there are concerns that it could exacerbate economic inequality. Those who control AI technology and data could wield significant power, widening the gap between the rich and the poor.

- **Cybersecurity Risks**: As AI systems are integrated into various sectors, they become potential targets for cyber attacks. AI-powered malware and hacking tools could be more sophisticated and difficult to detect.
- **Human Dependency on AI**: With increasing reliance on AI for decision-making and tasks, there is a risk of humans becoming overly dependent on AI systems. This could lead to a loss of critical thinking skills and autonomy.

Threat to jobs

There are many jobs that are currently (as of April, 2024) paying and are employing many people. You may be one such, currently earning money working on one of these jobs listed below. or may know some one working in such a job. Listing them out as the jobs with these tasks that will not exist in future (some in very near future and some not so far away) are not to be treated with panic. The idea of listing them herein is to prepare you for an eventuality. Best sought reaction is to work towards better preparing yourself to be relevant. Many of you reading this may even have employed people to the tasks mentioned herein and yes, the smartest of you would have already looking at technology alternates and those driven by AI.

Historically, such changes have been approached by employees with disdain and hatred towards employers. Even many governments have looked at this as a 'wrong' done towards the weaker section (the employees). Please, stop and think back the businesses or enterprises stopped from adopting new technologies though temporarily kept the same number of employees have eventually shut shop. While, those who let go some employees and adopted to new technology developments have grown big enough to create far more jobs in future.

Software industry

The software industry, despite being a driver of AI innovation, is not immune to job displacement due to automation and AI. Here are some job categories within the software industry that could potentially be impacted:

1. **Software Testers**: Testers roles have significantly come down in the last 2 decades with lots of automation seen in this space. AI-driven testing tools can automate test case generation, execution, and analysis, reducing the need for manual testing efforts, to the next level by further reducing the resources employed for this task.
2. **Technical Support Specialists**: AI-powered chatbots and virtual assistants have already started displacing tech support resources and have started eliminating the Level-0 and Level-1 support staffs. Going forward, AI powered technologies can handle customer inquiries and troubleshoot technical issues, reducing the need for human technical support even at Level -2 and Level-3.
3. **Quality Assurance Analysts**: Automation over a period of time has already been impacting this role for sometime and AI can automate quality assurance tasks, such as code reviews and performance testing, impacting roles of QA analysts for manual testing totally.
4. **Database Administrators**: AI can optimise database management tasks, automate performance tuning, and enhance data security, impacting roles of DBAs for routine maintenance. This is already in place across small and medium enterprises because of Cloud services providers. AI will now take these jobs out of larger enterprises as well.
5. **System Administrators**: AI-driven systems can automate system monitoring, configuration management, and troubleshooting, reducing the need for manual administration

tasks. This has also been in use for sometime that already there are more certified system administrators than jobs.

6. **Data Entry Operators**: AI can automate data entry tasks and data cleansing processes, reducing the need for manual data entry. This has been a work in progress for a few decades reducing resource dependency significantly and perhaps in the next decade this task will become totally irrelevant.

7. **Software Developers**: Low code and No code service providers have started impacting this task to some extent and going forward, AI is not likely to replace software developers entirely, it can assist in code generation, bug fixing, and code optimisation, will be impacting roles for certain programming tasks.

8. **Project Managers**: This may be the most hated or joked about role in a software development company but this is not a joke. AI will assist in project planning, resource allocation, and risk management, potentially impacting roles of project managers for routine tasks and significantly.

9. **UI/UX Designers**: AI-powered design tools can assist in generating user interfaces and user experience prototypes, impacting roles of designers for initial design phases. You are likely to think that I am far more creative and I know who will be loosing their jobs. Well, prepare yourself to start collaborating with AI companies to make these tools effective.

10. **Technical Writers**: Automation in this space has been a work in progress for some time and reaching the crescendo with AI is not far. AI-driven natural language generation tools can automate documentation tasks, such as generating user manuals and API documentation, reducing the need for manual technical writing. Writers skills needs to be powered with tool skills.

11. **DevOps Engineers**: AI can automate deployment pipelines, continuous integration processes, and infrastructure man-

agement, impacting roles of DevOps engineers for routine tasks. You don't want to accept this, I understand. Its coming, get prepared.

12. **Release Managers**: AI can assist in release planning, version control, and change management, impacting roles of release managers for coordinating software releases. People skills and customer and business understanding with tool skills will be the anchors for those who carry these roles in future.

13. **Network Administrators**: AI-driven network management tools can optimise network configurations, troubleshoot connectivity issues, and enhance security, impacting roles of network administrators for routine tasks. Some of you already know, these functions are already at play in some ecosystems. This will only consume more such jobs.

14. **Software Architects**: AI can assist in architectural design decisions, code pattern recognition, and scalability planning, impacting roles of software architects for certain design aspects. Debate remains, will the AI take the solution architects job or the technical architects job? I think both and depending on the cases.

15. **Localisation Specialists**: AI-powered language translation tools can assist in software localisation, reducing the need for manual translation efforts. This is already happening and tools skill will be the differentiator for those who want to find a pay cheque for a longer time.

16. **Automation Engineers**: AI can automate test scripts, build processes, and deployment tasks, impacting roles of automation engineers for routine automation. This is one of the roles which finds itself in the threat list but down the list for sure.

AI may impact these roles, it also creates new opportunities in fields such as AI engineering, data science, machine learning, and more. The future of work in the software industry will likely involve a shift towards roles that require human creativity, critical thinking, problem-solving skills, and a deep understanding of AI technologies to complement automation and AI-driven processes. Another area that is already collaborating with this space is the behavioural sciences.

Medical and Health care Community

17. **Radiologists**: AI-powered image analysis systems can assist in interpreting medical images, potentially reducing the need for human radiologists for routine scans. Automation and improving image processing technologies in the past few years will drive the large scale adoption soon.
18. **Pathologists**: AI algorithms can analyse pathology slides and assist in diagnosing diseases, impacting roles of pathologists for routine analysis.
19. **Medical Transcriptionists**: AI-driven speech recognition systems can transcribe medical dictations more accurately and quickly, reducing the need for manual transcription. This is one of the earliest tasks to get impacted and it continues to shrink.
20. **Pharmacists**: AI can assist in medication management, drug interactions, and prescription fulfilment, potentially impacting roles of pharmacists for routine tasks. Automation driven by Iot technologies will further get amplified with AI and the change will be faster than one can assume.
21. **Nurses and Caregivers**: AI-powered robots can assist with patient monitoring, medication reminders, and basic patient care, reducing the need for human caregivers for routine tasks. Robot caregivers are already being tested in Japan will change the approach to care giving in a manner that was never imagined till date. Also, considering the research that

suggests caregivers life span is getting reduced, these technology options become all the more necessary to hasten.

Agriculture

22. **Farm Workers**: AI-driven drones and robots can assist with planting, monitoring crops, and harvesting, reducing the need for manual labor. Mechanisation and automation had already brought in technology to farms and AI will only amplify and contribute to effective food security. These workers will have to acquire other skills and there will be more jobs around these.
23. **Crop Consultants**: AI-powered systems can provide real-time data on soil conditions, pest infestations, and crop health, impacting roles of crop consultants for field inspections. This has been going on with basic communication and digital solutions for some time now and the scope will get a huge booster with AI. The roles will change to SME's for some to work with technology providers and some will have to take on other such roles in the different value cycles of the crops.
24. **Agricultural Scientists**: AI can analyse agricultural data to optimise crop yields and sustainability, impacting roles of agricultural scientists for data analysis. They will have to acquire tool skills to be relevant and also help with developing and refining algorithms to be able to better work with communities around the farms and market interactions.

Food industry

25. **Food Production and Processing**: AI-driven robotics and automation systems can optimise food production processes, including planting, harvesting, sorting, and packaging. While AI may reduce the need for manual labor in

certain aspects of food production, human workers will still be required for oversight, maintenance, and quality control.
26. **Supply Chain Management**: AI-powered algorithms and predictive analytics can optimise supply chain logistics, inventory management, and demand forecasting in the food industry. While AI may improve supply chain efficiency, human professionals will still be needed for decision-making, negotiation, and coordination across various stakeholders.
27. **Menu Planning and Recipe Development**: AI algorithms can analyse food trends, ingredient combinations, and nutritional data to assist chefs and food developers in creating innovative menus and recipes. While AI may enhance menu planning efficiency, human chefs and culinary experts will still be valued for their creativity, taste, and expertise.
28. **Food Safety and Quality Control**: AI-driven sensors, monitoring devices, and quality assurance systems can detect contaminants, pathogens, and spoilage in food products. While AI may improve food safety standards, human inspectors and technicians will still be required for regulatory compliance, testing, and verification.
29. **Restaurant Operations**: AI-powered point-of-sale (POS) systems, inventory management software, and customer relationship management (CRM) platforms can streamline restaurant operations and enhance customer experiences. While AI may automate certain tasks, human restaurant staff will still be needed for customer service, food preparation, and hospitality.
30. **Food Delivery and Logistics**: AI-driven delivery algorithms, route optimisation software, and autonomous vehicles can improve efficiency and reliability in food delivery services. While AI may optimise delivery routes, human drivers and delivery personnel will still be required for navi-

gation, customer interaction, and order fulfilment for some more time. While robot and drone delivery will eventually get mature with AI systems and perhaps within the next 10 years.

31. **Customer Service and Support**: AI-powered chatbots, virtual assistants, and voice recognition systems can handle customer inquiries, process orders, and provide personalised recommendations in food service establishments. While AI may enhance customer service efficiency, human employees will still be valued for their empathy, communication skills, and problem-solving abilities.

32. **Food Retail and Merchandising**: AI-powered recommendation engines, dynamic pricing algorithms, and personalised marketing campaigns can enhance customer engagement and sales in food retail environments. While AI may optimise retail strategies, human employees will still be needed for product selection, merchandising, and customer interaction.

33. **Restaurant Reservations and Table Management**: AI-driven reservation systems, seating algorithms, and waitlist optimisation tools can improve restaurant efficiency and capacity management. While AI may optimise reservation processes, human hosts and managers will still be required for guest interaction, seating arrangements, and customer satisfaction.

34. **Food Waste Reduction**: AI-powered analytics platforms and waste tracking systems can identify inefficiencies, minimise food waste, and optimise resource utilisation in the food industry. While AI may reduce food waste, human employees will still be needed for decision-making, problem-solving, and operational management.

Law and Order

35. **Predictive Policing**: AI algorithms can analyse crime data, patterns, and trends to predict potential criminal activity and allocate resources more effectively. While AI may improve predictive capabilities, human police officers will still be needed to interpret data, make decisions, and respond to incidents on the ground.
36. **Crime Investigation**: AI-powered forensic tools, facial recognition systems, and video analytics software can assist in criminal investigations by identifying suspects, analysing evidence, and reconstructing crime scenes. While AI may enhance investigative capabilities, human detectives and investigators will still be essential for gathering evidence, conducting interviews, and solving cases.
37. **Patrol and Surveillance**: AI-driven surveillance cameras, drones, and sensors can monitor public spaces, detect suspicious behaviour, and alert law enforcement agencies to potential threats. While AI may improve surveillance capabilities, human police officers will still be needed to respond to emergencies, apprehend suspects, and maintain public order.
38. **Traffic Management**: AI algorithms can optimise traffic flow, analyse traffic patterns, and predict congestion to improve road safety and reduce traffic accidents. While AI may enhance traffic management systems, human police officers will still be required to enforce traffic laws, conduct traffic stops, and respond to accidents.
39. **Emergency Response**: AI-powered dispatch systems can prioritise emergency calls, route responders efficiently, and provide real-time situational awareness to first responders. While AI may improve emergency response times, human police officers, firefighters, and paramedics will still be need-

ed to assess situations, provide assistance, and coordinate rescue efforts.
40. **Community Policing**: AI-driven community engagement platforms and social media monitoring tools can facilitate communication between law enforcement agencies and the public, gather feedback, and address community concerns. While AI may enhance community policing efforts, human police officers will still be essential for building relationships, addressing local issues, and fostering trust.
41. **Training and Education**: AI-powered simulators, virtual reality training modules, and online learning platforms can supplement traditional police training programs and provide realistic scenarios for skill development. While AI may improve training efficiency, human instructors and mentors will still be needed to provide guidance, feedback, and support to trainees.
42. **Administrative Tasks**: AI-powered administrative systems, data management tools, and workflow automation software can streamline paperwork, record-keeping, and administrative tasks within police departments. While AI may reduce the burden of administrative work, human staff will still be required for decision-making, policy implementation, and oversight.
43. **Crisis Negotiation**: AI-driven conversational agents and negotiation algorithms can assist in crisis situations by providing communication support and de-escalation techniques. While AI may augment crisis negotiation efforts, human negotiators and crisis intervention specialists will still be needed to build rapport, defuse tensions, and resolve conflicts peacefully.
44. **Ethical and Legal Considerations**: AI technologies raise important ethical and legal considerations in law enforcement, including issues related to privacy, bias, accountability, and transparency. Human police officers, policymakers, and

legal experts will play a crucial role in ensuring that AI applications in policing adhere to ethical standards and respect civil liberties.

45. **Crime Prevention and Deterrence**: AI algorithms can analyse data on crime hotspots, criminal networks, and social factors to develop strategies for crime prevention and deterrence. While AI may support crime prevention efforts, human law enforcement (Police) officers will still be responsible for implementing tactics, engaging with communities, and enforcing laws.
46. **Legal Research and Analysis**: AI-powered legal research platforms and natural language processing tools can assist lawyers, prosecutors, and judges in analysing case law, statutes, and legal documents. While AI may improve legal research efficiency, human legal professionals will still be needed for interpretation, argumentation, and decision-making.
47. **Courtroom Proceedings**: AI-driven transcription software, case management systems, and virtual courtrooms can streamline courtroom proceedings and reduce administrative burdens. While AI may improve courtroom efficiency, human judges, lawyers, and court personnel will still be required for adjudication, advocacy, and procedural oversight.
48. **Prison Management**: AI-driven predictive analytics and inmate management systems can assist in prison management by optimising resource allocation, assessing inmate risk levels, and facilitating rehabilitation programs. While AI may enhance prison operations, human corrections officers and staff will still be needed for security, supervision, and inmate interaction.
49. **Policy Development and Oversight**: AI technologies raise important ethical, legal, and policy considerations in law enforcement, including issues related to privacy, bias, accountability, and transparency. Human policymakers, legal experts,

and oversight bodies will play a crucial role in ensuring that AI applications in law enforcement adhere to ethical standards and respect civil liberties.
50. **Community Engagement and Relations**: AI-driven community engagement platforms and social media monitoring tools can facilitate communication between law enforcement agencies and the public, gather feedback, and address community concerns. While AI may support community policing efforts, human law enforcement officers will still be essential for building trust, addressing local issues, and fostering positive relationships.

Armed Forces

51. **Soldiers**: Much of the analysis of Russian and Ukraine war has involved the strength of ground forces. Strength of NATO and Russia are measured not entirely but still on number of ground forces. Which is more of old habits and not true if one observes the technology advances each are making in the security space. For a long time, many countries have even been using outsourced man power for soldiers and even special forces as some call them Mercenaries. No country would like to see their citizens die and that casualty can cause the loss of power to the people in the government. This is where, AI technology and robots and other technologies will significantly displace human soldiers.
52. **Drone Operators**: With the rise of autonomous drones, roles of drone operators in the military could be impacted. This may not be immediate but clearly this will not be relevant for long.
53. **Military Analysts**: AI can analyse vast amounts of military data for strategic planning and threat assessment, impacting roles of military analysts for data analysis. They may still find roles to be the simulator strategists to educate the AI. Clear-

ly, this function will be around for sometime but will demand more creative thinking as wars are not necessarily fought with munitions or rather, munitions have changed forms from guns and missiles to ransomeware, malware, malicious apps, phishing, and host of other such threats.

54. **Logistics and Supply Officers**: AI can optimise military logistics, inventory management, and supply chain operations, impacting roles of supply officers for planning. There is significant automation in this space already and this will further get amplified by AI.

Hospitality

55. **Hotel Receptionists**: AI-powered chatbots and virtual assistants are already handling guest inquiries and bookings, reducing the need for human receptionists for routine tasks in few large or speciality hotels. While, some hotels even have robots and automation is very high. As AI prevalence is going to change the scenario even among the smaller players as well.
56. **Hotel Manager**: Staff less hotels are already becoming a thing and in the boutique hotels for now and the prevalence of AI systems will make it possible for all possible capacities.
57. **Concierge Services**: AI-driven systems can provide personalised recommendations and services to hotel guests, impacting roles of concierge services. Much of lot lead automation in this for sometime has been preparing the industry for the next phase with AI.

Academic

58. **Teachers and Educators**: AI-driven personalised learning platforms can provide tailored lessons and assessments to students, potentially impacting roles of teachers for curriculum delivery. While, there is a lot of argument on this, there

may be resistance at the primary schooling stage and at post graduation and above stages. Apart from this, the support staff are the first set of casualties here.
59. **Academic Researchers**: AI can assist in literature reviews, data analysis, and research tasks, impacting roles of academic researchers for data processing. Clearly, this function gets replaced by tools to the Academic staff and an area where students earning opportunity perhaps gets effected. For some, it may open up an opportunity if they champion the usage of AI tools.

Legal

60. **Lawyer/Attorney**: Lawyers, also known as attorneys, who essentially provide legal advice and representation to individuals, businesses, and organisations. Some of the specialisations, such as civil law, corporate law, intellectual property law, will be the earliest ones to find the roles challenged by AI. While there may be resistance to replace representation of clients in court proceedings, the function of drafting legal documents, negotiate settlements, and provide counsel on legal matters could well be seen by taken over by AI.
61. **Paralegals**: AI-powered platforms can assist with legal research, document review, and contract analysis, reducing the need for manual paralegal work. Initially the function may benefit with use of tools but in few years the very function could be replaced by AI.
62. **Legal Secretaries**: AI-driven tools can automate administrative tasks such as scheduling, document preparation, and case management, impacting roles of legal secretaries for routine tasks. As in paralegal, initially Legal secretaries will thrive when they champion the use of AI but in the next few years, they will find themselves replaced by more efficient AI systems.

63. **Judge/Magistrate**: Judges and magistrates preside over court proceedings and make legal decisions based on evidence presented by parties in a case. As much as one may argue otherwise, this function will start getting replaced by AI systems. This may not happen in all the cases but most likely it will start in lower courts within the next decade or so. As much as it may appear as science fiction, most of your generation of readers will see this day and for all you know, may even appreciate this, as this is certain to be consistent.
64. **Legal Counsel/In-House Counsel**: Legal counsel, also known as in-house counsel, are lawyers who work for corporations, government agencies, or non-profit organisations. Most of their functions including contracts, employment law, regulatory compliance, intellectual property, and such are the ones to be replaced by AI systems and please do not mistake them to robots. Litigation matters will continue though for a long time to come.
65. **Law Clerk**: Law clerks are typically law students or recent law school graduates who work for judges, law firms, or government agencies. They assist with legal research, drafting legal documents, and preparing case summaries. Law clerks gain valuable experience and insight into the legal profession while working under the supervision of experienced attorneys or judges. But, thats only one side of the function. For the law firms, judges and government agencies, they also mean cost and some times even poor research which could cost them lot more if they loose their case. Given that, its most likely one of the first functions to be replaced by AI systems.

Travel and Transport

66. **Airline Pilots**: With the development of autonomous aircraft, roles of airline pilots could be impacted. For quite some time,

in the advanced countries, armed attacks have been undertaken through unmanned drones. They may have been piloted by drone operators sitting thousands of kilometres away, Even they shall be replaced.

67. **Flight Attendant**: Flight attendants, also known as cabin crew, provide customer service, safety demonstrations, and emergency assistance to passengers on commercial flights. All these functions are easily displaced by the currently available digital display systems and robots and once amplified by AI, they will not be missed at all. How long? Will these jobs be relevant is anybody's guess.

68. **Airline Operations Manager**: Airline operations managers oversee the day-to-day operations of an airline, including flight scheduling, crew management, aircraft maintenance, and ground operations. They ensure that flights operate safely, efficiently, and on schedule. All of these functions can well be done far more efficiently by AI systems. To extend their relevance, these functions will have to learn to use AI tools but its matter of time these roles get displaced by AI systems.

69. **Air Traffic Controller**: Air traffic controllers monitor and coordinate the movement of aircraft in the airspace and on the ground. They provide instructions to pilots to ensure safe and orderly air traffic flow and prevent collisions. When, planes fly without pilots, its anybody's guess on the relevance of the Air Traffic controllers. AI will make them far more reliable and these functions like most other functions will need to have AI tool skills for sometime before they become irrelevant. Our political and compliance systems may necessitate these roles a bit longer than necessary.

70. **Travel Agent**: Travel agents assist clients in planning and booking travel arrangements, including flights, accommodations, transportation, and activities. Most of these functions got displaced already with online ticket booking services.

With AI, those who operate behind the scene for online ticketing services and a few who survived offering customised services also will get displaced by AI and customers will be happy with this.

71. **Tour Guide**: Tour guides lead groups of tourists on sightseeing tours, providing information about historical sites, landmarks, cultural attractions, and local customs. In most places they started getting displaced by headphones with coordinated audio systems and then digital systems enabled to communicate with sensor based IOT systems. With AI systems, what ever is left will also become a thing of the past.
72. **Transportation Planner**: Transportation planners develop and implement strategies for efficient and sustainable transportation systems, including roads, public transit, and rail networks. They analyse traffic patterns, conduct feasibility studies, and recommend infrastructure improvements. With time, these functions will necessarily start using AI tools and eventually ai system will displace this function as well.
73. **Logistics Coordinator**: Logistics coordinators manage the movement and storage of goods and materials, coordinating shipments, managing inventory, and optimising supply chain operations. AI tools will start making these jobs easier and in a short time, will displace them as well.
74. **Cruise Ship Staff**: Cruise ship staff work in various roles onboard cruise ships, including hospitality, food service, entertainment, and guest services. They provide amenities and services to passengers during their cruise vacation. Some of these functions will get displaced by AI and those depending on complexities that are entangled with other departments will continue to suffer. Many of the systems will come from the staff less hotels powered ecosystem.
75. **Railway Conductor**: Railway conductors are responsible for the safe operation of trains, including passenger safety, tick-

et collection, and ensuring compliance with railway regulations. They may work for passenger or freight rail companies. While, already many rail systems are becoming staff free particularly conductor free. We will see the last generation of conductors and Ticket collectors.

76. **Bus and Taxi Drivers**: With the rise of autonomous vehicles, roles of bus and taxi drivers for routine routes will be impacted. We will see an accident free world and that will be driven by autonomous vehicles and that future is already here, in few countries at least as autonomous taxis. Rest of them are only a consequence and lot sooner than one imagines as in 2024.

Security

77. **Security Guard/Officer**: This function is primarily being associated with patrolling designated areas, monitoring surveillance equipment, and enforcing security policies and procedures to prevent theft, vandalism, or unauthorised access. All these functions are already reduced in dependency to technology, going forward with advanced AI systems, pretty much all the listed functions of this role will be taken over.
78. **Loss Prevention Specialist**: Loss prevention specialists work to prevent theft, fraud, and shrinkage in retail stores, warehouses, or other business environments. These roles with also be a casualty to ai systems, but in many places these will remain more as to provide with human touch to the customers rather than for these functions.
79. **Security Supervisor/Manager**: Security supervisors or managers oversee security operations and personnel, ensuring that security protocols are followed, and security risks are addressed effectively. This will remain for next few years. Thereafter their roles will have to be far more sophisticated in their ability to understand and communicate technology and

also their ability and empathy to engage customers and their concerns and not oversee personnel. You may have clearly taken note of the persona of this role demands versus the prevalent one.

80. **Surveillance Operators**: AI-powered surveillance systems can monitor and analyse video feeds for security threats, reducing the need for manual monitoring.
81. **Security Analysts**: AI can analyse cybersecurity threats and detect anomalies in network traffic, impacting roles of security analysts for threat detection.
82. **Information Security Analyst**: Information security analysts are responsible for protecting an organisation's digital assets and data from cyber threats, such as hacking, malware, or data breaches.
83. **Cybersecurity Engineer**: Ai systems will be better equipped to design, implement, and maintain security solutions to protect computer systems, networks, and software applications from cyber threats.
84. **Intelligence Analyst**: AI systems can collect, analyse, and disseminate intelligence information to support security operations and decision-making.
85. **Background verification / screening**: There are plenty of roles under this, which will no longer be relevant with AI system. In the near future, a few roles will get created to manage AI tools but consequentially, much of those jobs will also be displaced by AI systems.

Construction

86. **Surveying**: AI and drone technology can automate land surveying tasks, such as collecting topographic data and creating maps, reducing the need for manual surveying work. Much of it is already in practice and very soon this will be the only way surveying gets done.

87. **Estimating**: AI algorithms can analyse construction plans, materials, and labor costs to generate accurate cost estimates for construction projects, potentially reducing the need for manual quantity surveying tasks. Currently, this is part of decision support system for large corporations, soon this will be the way every construction company operates.
88. **Quality Control**: AI-powered sensors and cameras can monitor construction sites for defects, safety hazards, and quality issues, providing real-time feedback to construction managers and reducing the need for manual inspection tasks. This function will not only eliminates jobs, it will also end a few businesses unless they pivot.
89. **Design and Planning**: AI software can assist architects and engineers in generating design options, optimising building layouts, and simulating structural performance, streamlining the design process and reducing reliance on manual drafting and modelling. For some time AI tool skill will be a differentiator for some of the architects before which this will be completely eliminated.

Manufacturing

90. **Assembly Line Worker**: AI-powered robots and automated systems can be used to perform repetitive assembly tasks, such as picking and placing components or soldering circuit boards, reducing the need for manual assembly line workers. Many manufacturing facilities for decades are now robot operated. The maturity in AI systems will make it far more affordable for even small manufacturing businesses with in the next decade.
91. **Machine Operation**: AI-controlled machines and robotic systems can automate manufacturing processes such as

machining, welding, and 3D printing, increasing productivity and reducing the need for manual machine operators.
92. **Quality Inspection**: AI-powered vision systems and machine learning algorithms can perform automated quality inspections of products, identifying defects or deviations from quality standards more accurately and efficiently than human inspectors. For the next 10 years, many businesses will have people with AI tool skills as specialists aided by AI tools to offer QA service, before being completely replaced by AI systems.
93. **Data Analysis**: AI algorithms can analyse production data, sensor readings, and machine performance metrics to optimise manufacturing processes, predict equipment failures, and improve overall production efficiency. Much of this has been a work in progress in aerospace and other critical industries and AI systems maturity will bring this to every other manufacturing industry within the next ten years.
94. **Inventory Management**: AI-powered inventory management systems can optimise inventory levels, forecast demand, and automate replenishment processes, reducing the need for manual inventory control and management tasks.

Entertainment

We will perhaps see retired or even dead actors being featured in new films portraying modern avatars and timelines they personally never lived to see or experienced. Needless to say, even dead musicians and singers will be making big comeback in the near future and entertaining new generations in a manner only AI could make it possible.

95. **Content Recommendation Algorithm**: AI-powered recommendation algorithms can analyse user preferences, viewing habits, and demographic data to personalise content recommendations on streaming platforms, reducing the need

for manual curation by human editors. These are already employed significantly by a few large corporations and the maturity of AI technology will make it available for smaller players as well.

96. **Visual Effects Rendering**: AI-driven software tools can automate the process of rendering visual effects, such as CGI (computer-generated imagery) and digital compositing, accelerating the production process and reducing the need for manual labor by VFX artists. Like many other jobs, these roles will benefit in the very near future with resources with AI tool skills getting more opportunities. With in the next 6 to 8 years, these jobs will not be relevant anymore.

97. **Music Composers**: AI algorithms can generate original music compositions or remix existing songs based on predefined criteria and style preferences, reducing the need for human composers and musicians in certain contexts. The contexts are also human bias and AI systems will be able to mimic the approach of legendary composers far superiorly than humans.

98. **Voice Synthesis**: AI-powered voice synthesis technology can replicate human speech patterns and generate lifelike voiceovers for audio narration, character dialogue, and virtual assistants, reducing the need for human voice actors in some applications. These systems are already in use for basic product demo videos and are also employed for customised content delivery. Popular voice can be generated without the person and pretty much eliminating the role of voice over artistes.

99. **Data Analytics**: AI-powered analytics platforms can analyse audience engagement, social media trends, and market dynamics to inform marketing strategies, audience targeting, and content distribution decisions, reducing the reliance on human analysts.

100. **Video Editors**: AI-driven editing tools can assist in video production and editing, reducing the need for manual editing work. For the next few years, perhaps Video editors with AI tool skills will thrive, before they find themselves out of job. As AI systems will be able to personalise content even at the edit level to make it available to the consumer choice. Same film can be available for 100 mins to 150 minis, depending on the demography of the audiences.

Utilities

101. **Power Plant Operators**: AI-driven systems can optimise power generation and distribution, impacting roles of power plant operators for monitoring and control. Most the power plants as such employ significant amount of automation and with increased number of nuclear power plants coming up in India specifically and also across the globe, AI systems application to ensure safety and security of people and also potential sabotage is an eventuality.
102. **Meter Reading and Data Collection**: AI-powered smart meters and sensors can automate the collection of utility usage data, reducing the need for manual meter reading by field technicians. This could impact roles such as meter readers and data collectors. These are already part of the government mandate in many places within India and internationally.
103. **Predictive Maintenance**: AI algorithms can analyse sensor data from utility infrastructure to predict equipment failures and schedule maintenance proactively, reducing the need for reactive maintenance by field technicians and maintenance crews.
104. **Grid Optimisation**: AI-based grid optimisation software can analyse energy consumption patterns, optimise grid operations, and manage renewable energy sources more efficient-

ly. This could impact roles related to grid management, operations, and dispatch. Already Smart grids employ most of the technology to facilitate this.
105. **Customer Service**: AI-powered chatbots and virtual assistants can handle customer inquiries, billing issues, and service requests, reducing the need for human customer service representatives in call centres and support centres.
106. **Asset Management**: AI systems can analyse data from sensors and IoT devices to optimise asset performance, extend asset lifespan, and prioritise investment decisions. This could impact roles related to asset management, maintenance planning, and capital projects.
107. **Energy Trading and Market Analysis**: AI algorithms can optimise energy trading strategies based on market trends, demand forecasts, and regulatory requirements. This could impact roles related to energy trading, risk management, and market analysis.
108. **Water Quality Monitoring**: AI-based analytics platforms can analyse water quality data to monitor contamination levels, detect leaks, and optimise water treatment processes. This could impact roles related to water quality monitoring, water treatment, and environmental compliance.
109. **Supply Chain Management**: AI-powered supply chain management systems can optimise inventory levels, streamline logistics operations, and reduce costs in the procurement and distribution of utility supplies and equipment.
110. **Cybersecurity**: AI-driven cybersecurity tools can detect and respond to cyber threats in real-time, protecting utility infrastructure from cyberattacks and data breaches. This could impact roles related to cybersecurity operations, incident response, and security compliance. Many other similar roles are are discussed under security and Software as well.

Facilities

111. **Facilities Managers**: AI can optimise building operations, maintenance schedules, and energy efficiency, impacting roles of facilities managers for planning. Like Hotel managers, for next few years these roles will be handled by people who have AI tools skill before which they will be displaced by AI.

112. **Predictive Maintenance**: AI algorithms can analyse sensor data from building systems and equipment to predict maintenance needs and identify potential issues before they occur. This could reduce the need for reactive maintenance and impact roles such as maintenance technicians and field engineers.

113. **Energy Management**: AI-powered energy management systems can optimise building HVAC (heating, ventilation, and air conditioning) systems, lighting, and other energy-consuming devices to reduce energy consumption and costs. This could impact roles related to energy management and sustainability.

114. **Space Utilisation**: AI analytics platforms can analyse occupancy data, foot traffic patterns, and space utilisation metrics to optimise space allocation and layout in buildings. This could impact roles related to space planning and utilisation analysis. This is one such space which will be driven by new businesses who will use AI tools offering this as a service by displacing in-house resources and subsequently the maturity of AI systems will also kill these businesses as well.

115. **Facility Security**: AI-driven security systems can monitor building entrances, detect unauthorised access, and analyse video surveillance footage to enhance security measures. This could impact roles related to security monitoring and access control. Much of this and more are covered under security.

116. **Cleaning and Janitorial Services**: AI-powered cleaning robots and autonomous floor scrubbers can automate routine cleaning tasks, such as vacuuming and mopping floors, reducing the need for manual labor by janitorial staff. Such products have already been in use in homes for sometime and soon will be available for large scale application, including roads and public infrastructure cleaning powered by AI systems.
117. **Inventory Management**: AI-powered inventory management systems can track and manage supplies, equipment, and spare parts in facilities, reducing inventory costs and minimising stockout. This could impact roles related to inventory control and procurement.
118. **Work Order Management**: AI-driven work order management systems can prioritise and schedule maintenance tasks, assign resources efficiently, and track work order status in real-time. This could impact roles related to work order coordination and dispatch.
119. **Tenant Services**: AI-powered virtual assistants and chatbots can provide tenants with information, assistance, and support services, reducing the need for human interaction in tenant management and customer service roles.

Waste Management

120. **Route Optimisation**: AI algorithms can analyse data on waste generation, collection points, and traffic patterns to optimise collection routes and schedules. This could reduce the need for manual route planning by waste collection drivers.
121. **Automated Sorting**: AI-powered sorting systems can identify and separate recyclable materials from mixed waste streams using sensors, cameras, and machine learning algorithms. This could reduce the need for manual sorting by

workers at recycling facilities. AI systems make the process efficient but also safer.

122. **Predictive Maintenance**: AI algorithms can monitor equipment performance, detect anomalies, and predict maintenance needs for waste collection trucks, sorting machines, and other infrastructure. This could reduce downtime and maintenance costs for waste management facilities.

123. **Bin Monitoring**: AI sensors and IoT (Internet of Things) devices can monitor waste bin fill levels, detect overflow conditions, and optimise collection frequencies. This could reduce unnecessary pickups and improve operational efficiency.

124. **Landfill Management**: AI analytics platforms can analyse data on landfill capacity, waste composition, and environmental factors to optimise landfill operations and minimise environmental impact. This could reduce the need for manual oversight and monitoring of landfill sites.

125. **Waste Tracking and Reporting**: AI-powered systems can track the movement of waste materials from collection to disposal, generate reports on waste volumes and composition, and ensure regulatory compliance. This could streamline administrative tasks and reporting requirements for waste management companies.

126. **Robotic Waste Collection**: AI-powered robots and autonomous vehicles can collect and transport waste materials from bins to collection trucks or sorting facilities, reducing the need for manual labor by waste collection workers.

127. **Waste-to-Energy Conversion**: AI algorithms can optimise the conversion of organic waste into energy through processes such as anaerobic digestion or incineration. This could improve energy recovery efficiency and reduce greenhouse gas emissions from waste disposal.

Sports

128. **Sports Analysts**: AI can analyse sports data for performance insights and strategy optimisation, impacting roles of sports analysts for data analysis. There have been analytical tools and currently these tool skills make it very important for these sports analysts and going forward, they will need AI tool skills to function effectively in these roles. Eventually AI systems will displace this function as well as businesses focused at providing this as a service.
129. **Data Analysis and Performance Optimisation**: AI algorithms can analyse vast amounts of data on athlete performance, training regimens, game strategies, and opponent scouting to provide insights and recommendations for improving athletic performance. This could impact roles such as sports analysts, performance coaches, and sports scientists.
130. **Scouting and Talent Identification**: AI-powered analytics platforms can analyse player statistics, biometric data, and video footage to identify talented athletes and potential recruits for sports teams. This could impact roles related to talent scouting, player recruitment, and talent management.
131. **Injury Prevention and Rehabilitation**: AI algorithms can analyse bio-mechanical data, injury histories, and rehabilitation protocols to develop personalised injury prevention programs and accelerate recovery for injured athletes. This could impact roles such as sports medicine physicians, physical therapists, and athletic trainers. In the near term some of the businesses offering this service will use AI tools and like everything else, this will also be displaced eventually.
132. **Fan Engagement and Personalisation**: AI-powered chatbots, virtual assistants, and personalised content recommendation systems can enhance fan engagement by providing tailored experiences, interactive content, and real-time

updates on favourite teams and athletes. This could impact roles in sports marketing, fan engagement, and digital media. In the near term some of the businesses offering this service will use AI tools and like everything else, this will also be displaced eventually.
133. **Broadcasting and Content Production**: AI-driven video production tools can automate the editing, tagging, and distribution of sports content, such as highlights, replays, and analysis segments. This could impact roles in sports broadcasting, video editing, and content creation.
134. **Ticketing and Venue Management**: AI-powered ticketing platforms can optimise ticket pricing, seating arrangements, and venue operations to enhance the fan experience and maximise revenue for sports events. This could impact roles in ticket sales, venue management, and event operations.
135. **Sports Equipment Design and Manufacturing**: AI algorithms can optimise the design, materials, and performance characteristics of sports equipment, such as athletic footwear, apparel, and gear. This could impact roles in sports product design, research and development, and manufacturing.
136. **Sports Betting and Gaming**: AI-powered predictive analytics platforms can analyse sports data and betting trends to inform betting strategies and odds-making for sports betting operators. This could impact roles in sports betting analysis, risk management, and trading.
137. **Athlete Representation and Negotiation**: AI algorithms can analyse contract terms, market trends, and player performance metrics to optimise contract negotiations and maximise earnings for athletes and sports agents. This could impact roles in sports agent representation, contract negotiation, and athlete management.

Event management

138. **Event Planners**: AI-powered event planning platforms can automate tasks such as venue selection, vendor coordination, and scheduling, impacting roles of event planners for routine tasks.
139. **Event Photographers**: AI-driven image editing tools can enhance event photos and automate editing processes, impacting roles of event photographers for post-production work.
140. **Event Planning and Coordination**: AI-powered event planning platforms can automate tasks such as venue selection, budgeting, scheduling, and logistics coordination. This could reduce the need for manual labor by event planners and coordinators.
141. **Attendee Engagement and Personalisation**: AI-driven chatbots, virtual assistants, and recommendation engines can personalise event experiences, provide real-time assistance to attendees, and facilitate networking opportunities. This could impact roles related to attendee engagement and customer service.
142. **Marketing and Promotion**: AI algorithms can analyse data on attendee preferences, behaviour patterns, and social media interactions to optimise marketing strategies, target advertising campaigns, and maximise ticket sales. This could impact roles in event marketing, digital advertising, and social media management.
143. **Ticketing and Registration**: AI-powered ticketing platforms can automate ticket sales, registration processes, and attendee check-ins using facial recognition and biometric authentication technologies. This could reduce the need for manual ticketing and registration staff.
144. **Venue Management**: AI systems can optimise venue layouts, seating arrangements, and crowd flow management to

enhance the attendee experience and maximise space utilisation. This could impact roles related to venue operations and facilities management.
145. **Content Curation and Programming**: AI algorithms can analyse content trends, audience preferences, and speaker profiles to curate event agendas, select keynote speakers, and schedule breakout sessions. This could impact roles in content curation, speaker management, and program development.
146. **Live Streaming and Virtual Events**: AI-driven streaming platforms can produce high-quality live broadcasts, virtual events, and hybrid experiences using automated camera systems, real-time editing software, and interactive features. This could impact roles in event production, audiovisual (AV) technology, and livestream management.
147. **Data Analytics and Insights**: AI-powered analytics platforms can analyse event data, feedback surveys, and attendee engagement metrics to generate actionable insights, measure event ROI, and inform decision-making. This could impact roles in data analysis, business intelligence, and reporting.
148. **On-Site Support and Technical Assistance**: AI-powered kiosks, self-service stations, and interactive displays can provide on-site support, way-finding assistance, and information services to attendees without the need for human staff.
149. **Event Security and Safety**: AI-driven surveillance systems, facial recognition technology, and predictive analytics can enhance event security measures, identify potential threats, and mitigate risks in real-time. This could impact roles in event security, risk management, and emergency response.

Fitness

150. **Fitness Instructors**: AI-driven fitness apps and wearable devices can provide personalised workout plans and feedback, reducing the need for in-person fitness instructors for routine training. For some time now, this has been available in few cities and through few large and expensive brands. With AI systems getting mature, they will also be affordable and with the amount of digitisation thats underway, personal fitness instructors will be the only job and for those who can afford.

151. **Personal Training**: AI-powered fitness apps and virtual trainers can provide personalised workout plans, exercise demonstrations, and real-time feedback to users. While AI may complement the work of human personal trainers, it could potentially reduce the demand for in-person training sessions. Personal training will become a premium service as mentioned earlier and AI based service will be for everybody.

152. **Group Fitness Instruction**: AI-driven virtual group fitness classes and interactive workout experiences can offer engaging alternatives to traditional instructor-led classes. This could impact roles in group fitness instruction, although human instructors may still be preferred for certain classes and formats.

153. **Fitness Facility Management**: AI systems can optimise gym operations, track equipment usage, and manage facility maintenance to improve efficiency and member satisfaction. This could reduce the need for manual oversight and administrative tasks by gym managers and staff.

154. **Nutrition Counselling**: AI-powered nutrition apps and dietary analysis tools can offer personalised meal plans, nutritional guidance, and calorie tracking features to users. While AI may assist individuals in managing their diets, human nutritionists and dieticians may still be sought after for person-

alised advice and support. Few app based services have started it and this will get a lot mature and dominate significantly in near future.
155. **Wearable Fitness Technology**: AI-driven wearable devices and fitness trackers can monitor physical activity, track vital signs, and provide real-time health insights to users. While AI may enhance the functionality of wearable devices, human experts may still be needed to interpret and act on the data collected.
156. **Wellness Coaching**: AI-powered wellness platforms and virtual coaching services can offer lifestyle advice, stress management techniques, and mental health support to users. While AI may provide valuable resources for wellness coaching, human coaches and counsellors may still be preferred for personalised guidance and empathy.
157. **Rehabilitation and Physical Therapy**: AI-driven rehabilitation devices and tele-therapy platforms can assist individuals in recovering from injuries, surgeries, and chronic conditions. While AI may augment the rehabilitation process, human physical therapists and healthcare professionals may still play a critical role in patient care and supervision. Even though Technology may become more effective, compliance and politics are two primary aspects which will delay the complete takeover of AI systems in this space.
158. **Fitness Content Creation**: AI algorithms can generate workout routines, exercise videos, and fitness content for online platforms and social media channels. While AI may automate content creation to some extent, human fitness influencers and content creators may still be valued for their expertise and authenticity.
159. **Fitness Equipment Design and Manufacturing**: AI-driven design software and predictive analytics can optimise the design, ergonomics, and performance of fitness equipment. While AI may streamline the product development process,

human engineers and designers may still be needed for innovation and quality control.
160. **Fitness Marketing and Sales**: AI-powered marketing automation tools and customer relationship management (CRM) systems can optimise lead generation, customer engagement, and sales conversions in the fitness industry. While AI may improve marketing efficiency, human marketers and sales professionals may still be essential for building relationships and driving revenue.

Preparing for Artificial Intelligence?

We have gone through the history and evolution of AI. We have also understood the use case and its applications and more importantly the skills required to further contribute to the development and application of AI across various sectors. In this essay I am trying to approach the evolution and most importantly our preparations for the future of AI. Every time we talk about future, there is a reference to how AI will be impacting our future. Hence, I will want to step back to how we as human beings have prepared ourselves over the course of history for the present day and the future. Thereby want to approach how we should prepare for the future with AI.

Humour me for a while, Every time there is a new Technology or innovation that is bound to impact the humanity at large, the human population seem to divide into three categories;
1. The believers (of change)
2. The nay sayers (oppose change)
3. The followers (go with the loudest voice at that time)

Whats important to understand in this context is that these three categories of people are not separated by any solid wall but highly porous separator that facilitates easy movement of people across each of the categories and rather seamlessly.

Most often it is believed that the people who contribute to the change are those who drive the change or those belonging to "The Believers" category. It is not necessarily so. Time and again we have seen even among Scientists that people do course correct as they move forward and it is rightly so. Human being is a creature of 'choice' as much as habit.

Sometimes, the opportunity drives people from one category to another and sometimes the insecurity, these are applicable to both the category of people as much to "The believers" as much to the "the nay sayers". Most often "The followers" tend go between either of the groups and it is even fair to say that this category comprises a pool of people belonging to both the categories 1 and 2. They even act as the cheer leaders and are often swayed by

    a. Political aspects or
    b. Social aspects or
    c. Economic aspects

Which of these aspects influence at what point of time, depends on the influencers play and their leanings and agendas of the time and space. This is where, we can notice that Republican Party and Democratic Party (of USA) have changed their stands diametrically opposite to what were fundamental to them as a party and their followers at some time in history.

With this backdrop, I would like to bring to your notice that we as human beings have always been focused at governance. While we kept trying to develop new models and process to govern ourselves better and rather more efficiently. We have developed more religions and faiths and stitched our identities around them. Most of the countries have moved from Church-State model to Self governance and Democracy which is often projected as an alternate to Communism in fact provides Communism as an option with Communist party using democracy to govern in China to Communist party's participating in electoral politics of Democracy in many countries. Despite all that, including killings to uphold one's faith and the presumed superiority over the others its the sheer motivation to control power that has still ensured over 50 countries ruled by dictators or authoritarian regimes.

Despite all this, last few centuries is largely been driven by human beings ability to engage other human beings. In the last 100 years or so we are training humans to engage machines. As horses (and horse carriages) were replaced by Cars and we managed to put together Mechanical manuals and Traffic rules to use those cars more efficiently. The same approach got extended into every electronic devises that got into our work space or homes. Many of which we carry with us all through as watches or phones or tablets or even as implants in some cases. We have technical manuals for us as how to handle them and care for them. This has been our approach to evolution. Hope to make this clear through a depiction in an evolutionary sense.

Humanity's success depended on our ability to engage externalities at different points of evolutionary period;
1. Human Vs Plants (Farming)
2. Human Vs Animal (Hunting / Domestication)
3. Human Vs Community (Religion / Faith)
4. Human Vs State (Country / Region)
5. Human Vs Books (Information)
6. Human Vs Mechanics (Automobile)
7. Human Vs Electronics (Devices, Refrigerator, etc.)
8. Human Vs Computers (Data Analysis)
9. Human Vs Internet (E-Commerce, Connected world)
10. Human Vs Artificial Intelligence (?)

In the recent history, every business school across the globe have championed on teaching how to work with other people. It is for a long time said that the greatest skill one is required to have to succeed is her or his ability to engage other people. This has been the approach since the 6th evolutionary period from the above chart. Despite the technology evolution and which did change the way we prepared ourselves, this core philosophy has remained same.

With plants, we learned to understand the environment and how to grow and even in controlling aspects that impact their growth to suit our needs. Like wise, with animals, we learned to save ourselves and then to kill them to ensure we don't have to worry about saving yourselves all the time and then even to hunt them to feed ourselves to hunt them for sport. While, I would love to indulge into the 3rd, 4th and 5th evolutionary periods mentioned above I will skip them for this chapter, while hoping that I am still able to retain you as a reader this far.

Nearly 200 years ago the first instructional manual was ever put to use and since then we as human beings are always communicated with as to how to engage with a mechanical or electrical or an electronic device. This has become a standard feature ever since with every equipment or product that one buys or even a toy or furniture comes with an instruction manual as to how to assemble (incase of a DIY, product) to make it work to care for it, after use to extend its utility. Which did make our lives a lot better and even freed up a lot of our times, just so that we can put that time to anything we find constructive or useful or for nothing as a choice.

In the last 10 years, we have been getting more exposed to the possibilities of AI and the narratives are getting so strong that people tend to refer to AI for things remotely distant from them. Much of Machine learning has been credited with AI, which is still fine considering its within the realm. Much of the sensors applications have been referred to AI and thats very unfortunate but considering that it is generating curiosity on the develop-

ment of technology in general and AI in particular is the silver lining.
One question I want to bring up here is, Should we(humans) be preparing for AI? Answer unfortunately will be, yes. By most people and has been yes for the most informed people as well. Where is this coming from? Like the argument I made about our habit of getting an instruction manual that prepares us to set-up, use, care for the machines (mechanical or electrical or electronic) that mindset is helping us to prepare for as simple as
a. How to ask a query to google to get best results from google, to
b. How to ask a question to Alexa to Siri to Cortana to get the best output, to
c. How to ask the right prompts to get the best output from open AI

These are the kind of learnings we want our people to be trained with to master the technologies to get the best value from them. Most people and even enterprises do not think anything wrong with this approach. They make budgets to get their staff to be trained and even academic institutions offer programs as upskilling the resources to be more productive and use technology optimally.

Whats the argument?

Argument here is simple.

We had generations learn to engage people more effectively and this will always be the case.

We have been learning to engage with animals and we have championed them to such an extent that we have domesticated most aggressive hunting dogs and even trained cats to work for us (at least in Israel).

We have been getting last few generations of human beings to engage with machines and made rules to accommodate ourselves around machines as the technology so demanded and for the times we are in, accommodating still means convenience in larger sense to us.

Having a similar approach to future will be disastrous. Technology is getting a lot mature, Technologists are building far intelligent systems. We don't need to approach them in a manner of training ourselves (human beings) to live with them or engage them better to make them more efficient let alone not be a threat for ourselves. We need to make the systems empathetic to us (human beings) from the start. We need to train the autonomous cars that we will be driven by to recognise our emotions. Recognise our triggers for joy and irritable aspects we need machines to work beyond being censors. We need to train them to be empathetic. This demands our efforts to be more collaborative. We need AI architects to work with mechanics and also customer service folks and even customers. We need collaborative efforts to happen between AI architects, designers, and doctors, and medical equipment technicians, and people to address healthcare solutions and not create a system to sustain patient care. We need more studies to happen on decoding behavioural studies and not to write instruction manuals to sell fancy gadgets that one needs to work with but build products that comes to our work spaces and homes and schools and learns to be productive. Not the other way.

Is that even possible?

Yes, but we need to start thinking in that direction.

Lastly, I had mentioned at the start of this book; "the time for all of us to get trained with Pragmatic Creativity and or practice Creative pragmatism." Caring to explain the terms and hope it helps to bring all of us onto the same page.

Pragmatic creativity: This approach involves applying creative thinking within the constraints of practical considerations such as time, budget, and resources. It encourages us to seek innovative solutions that are both imaginative and feasible in real-world contexts. Pragmatic creativity allows for the exploration of unconventional ideas while ensuring they are actionable and effective.

Creative pragmatism: This approach involves incorporating practical considerations into the creative process to ensure that innovative ideas are implemented effectively. It encourages us to balance creativity with pragmatism by considering factors such as scalability, sustainability, and impact. Creative pragmatism enables us to turn creative visions into tangible results by aligning them with practical goals and constraints.

If not now, when else?

Reference materials - Books & Podcasts

Here is a list of recommended reference books covering various aspects of AI, including Generative AI, policy-making, skills development, business applications, ethics, and more:

Books
Artificial Intelligence (AI):
"**Artificial Intelligence: A Modern Approach**" by Stuart Russell and Peter Norvig
> A comprehensive textbook covering the fundamentals of AI, including problem-solving, knowledge representation, machine learning, and more.

"**Deep Learning**" by Ian Goodfellow, Yoshua Bengio, and Aaron Courville
> Focuses on deep learning, including neural networks, optimisation techniques, and applications in computer vision, natural language processing, and reinforcement learning.

"**Pattern Recognition and Machine Learning**" by Christopher M. Bishop
> Covers pattern recognition, machine learning concepts, and algorithms, with a focus on probabilistic graphical models and Bayesian methods.

Generative AI:
"**Generative Deep Learning: Teaching Machines to Paint, Write, Compose, and Play**" by David Foster
> Provides insights into Generative AI models such as GANs, VAEs, and autoregressive models, with practical examples in image generation, text generation, and more.

"**Generative Adversarial Networks: An Introduction**" by Oliver Dürr, Philip Bordes, and Jean-Christophe Zufferey
>Focuses on Generative Adversarial Networks (GANs), explaining their architecture, training methods, and applications in image and text generation.

Policy-making for AI:

"**The AI Policy Handbook**" by Jason Matheny and David Ferguson
>Offers guidance on policy development for AI, covering topics such as regulation, ethical considerations, international cooperation, and economic impact.

"**Ethics and Policies for Cyber Operations: A NATO Cooperative Cyber Defence Centre of Excellence Initiative**" by Mariarosaria Taddeo and Ludovica Glorioso
>Explores ethical and policy issues related to cyber operations, including AI applications, cybersecurity, privacy, and human rights.

Skills for AI:

"**Python for Data Analysis**" by Wes McKinney
>A practical guide to using Python for data analysis, including data manipulation, visualisation, and statistical analysis, essential for AI work.

"**Hands-On Machine Learning with Scikit-Learn, Keras, and TensorFlow**" by Aurélien Géron
>Teaches machine learning concepts and practical implementation using Scikit-Learn, Keras, and TensorFlow, with examples in regression, classification, and neural networks.

AI for Business:

"**AI Superpowers: China, Silicon Valley, and the New World Order**" by Kai-Fu Lee
>Explores the impact of AI on business and society, with insights into China's AI development, innovation, and implications for the global economy.

"**Competing in the Age of AI: Strategy and Leadership When Algorithms and Networks Run the World**" by Marco Iansiti and Karim R. Lakhani
>Discusses how businesses can leverage AI technologies for competitive advantage, covering strategy, organisational transformation, and AI-driven business models.

AI for Ethics:

"**Artificial Unintelligence: How Computers Misunderstand the World**" by Meredith Broussard
>Examines the ethical implications of AI, including biases, limitations, and societal impacts, with a focus on the importance of human oversight.

"**Robot Ethics: The Ethical and Social Implications of Robotics**" by Patrick Lin, Keith Abney, and Ryan Jenkins
>Explores ethical considerations in robotics and AI, including issues of responsibility, autonomy, privacy, and the impact of AI on society.

Cyber security:

The Perfect Weapon: War, Sabotage, and Fear in the Cyber Age by David E. Sanger

Countdown to Zero Day: Stuxnet and the Launch of the World's First Digital Weapon by Kim Zetter

Dark Territory: The Secret History of Cyber War by Fred Kaplan

Cyber War: The Next Threat to National Security and What to Do About It
by Richard A. Clarke and Robert K. Knake

Additional Recommendations:
"**Weapons of Math Destruction: How Big Data Increases Inequality and Threatens Democracy**" by Cathy O'Neil
> Explores the ethical implications of algorithms and AI in decision-making, highlighting issues of fairness, accountability, and transparency.

"**AI Ethics**" (The MIT Press Essential Knowledge series) by Mark Coeckelbergh
> Provides a concise overview of AI ethics, covering topics such as bias, privacy, accountability, and the social impact of AI technologies.

Podcasts

There are several excellent podcasts dedicated to AI that provide valuable insights, interviews with experts, discussions on latest trends, and updates in the field. Here are some recommended podcasts on AI to follow or subscribe to:

1. **Artificial Intelligence Podcast by Lex Friedman**
   - Host: Lex Fridman
   - Description: Conversations with researchers, engineers, and thought leaders in AI, covering a wide range of topics from deep learning to robotics to the impact of AI on society.
   - Link to Podcast

2. **Talking Machines**
   - Hosts: Katherine Gorman and Neil Lawrence

- Description: A podcast exploring the past, present, and future of AI and machine learning. Episodes include interviews with experts, discussions on latest research, and AI-related news.
- Link to Podcast

3. **AI in Business Podcast**
    - Host: Daniel Faggella
    - Description: Discussions on the business applications of AI, including interviews with business leaders, data scientists, and AI experts. Topics include AI adoption, ROI, and industry-specific use cases.
    - Link to Podcast

4. **TWIML AI Podcast (This Week in Machine Learning & AI)**
    - Host: Sam Charrington
    - Description: Features interviews with researchers, practitioners, and entrepreneurs in the AI and machine learning space. Covers topics such as deep learning, natural language processing, and AI ethics.
    - Link to Podcast

5. **Data Skeptic**
    - Host: Kyle Polich
    - Description: A podcast that explores concepts in data science, AI, and machine learning. Episodes cover topics like algorithms, data privacy, and AI applications in different industries.
    - Link to Podcast

6. **AI Today Podcast**
    - Hosts: Kathleen Walch and Ronald Schmelzer
    - Description: Focuses on the practical and ethical implications of AI technologies. Features discussions on AI trends,

adoption challenges, and use cases across various industries.
- Link to Podcast

7. The AI Alignment Podcast
- Host: Lucas Perry
- Description: Explores the philosophical, ethical, and technical challenges of aligning AI systems with human values. Features interviews with AI safety and ethics researchers.
- Link to Podcast

8. Machine Learning Guide
- Host: OCDevel (Ryan Harris)
- Description: A beginner-friendly podcast covering fundamental concepts of machine learning and AI. Episodes include explanations of algorithms, best practices, and practical tips.
- Link to Podcast

9. The AI Element Podcast
- Host: Dr. Chris Clack
- Description: A podcast focusing on AI and its impact on society, business, and everyday life. Covers topics such as AI ethics, explainability, and bias.
- Link to Podcast

10. Machine Learning Street Talk
- Hosts: Tim Scarfe, Yannic Kilcher, and Conor McDonald
- Description: A podcast discussing all things related to machine learning, including deep dives into research papers, interviews with researchers, and debates on various ML topics.
- Link to Podcast

11. **Making Data Simple**
    - Host: Al Martin
    - Description: Covers a range of topics related to data science and AI, including interviews with industry experts, discussions on AI ethics, and practical AI applications.
    - Link to Podcast

12. **The AI Ethics Podcast**
    - Hosts: CognitionX
    - Description: Explores the ethical implications of AI technologies, including fairness, bias, transparency, and responsible AI development.
    - Link to Podcast

Broadly about future:

1. **FutureFast Podcast**
    - Hosts: Palecanda Nanjunda Pratap (Author)
    - Description: Conversations with accomplished entrepreneurs, professionals, leaders from all aspects of business, technology and administration sharing their perspective on future.
    - Link to Podcast

2. This list has host of Podcasts on future that you can choose from and follow with.

https://www.bcast.fm/blog/best-futurist-podcasts

People who impacted and, continue to impact AI evolution and adoption.

Alan Turing : https://en.wikipedia.org/wiki/Alan_Turing

Allen Newell & Herbert Simon: https://en.wikipedia.org/wiki/Allen_Newell & https://en.wikipedia.org/wiki/Herbert_A._Simon

David Rumehart : https://en.wikipedia.org/wiki/David_Rumelhart

Geoffrey Hinton :
https://en.wikipedia.org/wiki/Geoffrey_Hinton

John McCarthy :
https://en.wikipedia.org/wiki/John_McCarthy_(computer_scientist)

Vladimir Vapnik :
https://en.wikipedia.org/wiki/Vladimir_Vapnik

Corinna Cortes :
https://en.wikipedia.org/wiki/Corinna_Cortes

Aravind Joshi : https://en.wikipedia.org/wiki/Aravind_Joshi

Ray Kurzweil : https://en.wikipedia.org/wiki/Ray_Kurzweil

Alex Krizhevsky : https://en.wikipedia.org/wiki/Alex_Krizhevsky

Ilya Sutskever : https://en.wikipedia.org/wiki/Ilya_Sutskever

Paul Smolensky : https://en.wikipedia.org/wiki/Paul_Smolensky

Shimon Ullman : https://en.wikipedia.org/wiki/Shimon_Ullman

James McClelland : https://en.wikipedia.org/wiki/James_McClelland_(psychologist)

Linda Smith : https://en.wikipedia.org/wiki/Linda_B._Smith

Judea Pearl : https://en.wikipedia.org/wiki/Judea_Pearl

Peter Dayan : https://en.wikipedia.org/wiki/Peter_Dayan

Yoshua Bengio : https://en.wikipedia.org/wiki/Yoshua_Bengio

Stuart J Russell : https://en.wikipedia.org/wiki/Stuart_J._Russell

Ian Goodfellow : https://en.wikipedia.org/wiki/Ian_Goodfellow

Kai-fu Lee : https://en.wikipedia.org/wiki/Kai-Fu_Lee

Stanislas Dehaene : https://en.wikipedia.org/wiki/Stanislas_Dehaene

Lila Gleitman : https://en.wikipedia.org/wiki/Lila_R._Gleitman

Nick Bostrom :
https://en.wikipedia.org/wiki/Nick_Bostrom

Michael Tomasello :
https://en.wikipedia.org/wiki/Michael_Tomasello

Pedro Domingos :
https://en.wikipedia.org/wiki/Pedro_Domingos

Dedre Gentner :
https://en.wikipedia.org/wiki/Dedre_Gentner

Peter Norvig : https://en.wikipedia.org/wiki/Peter_Norvig

Aaron Courville : https://mila.quebec/en/person/aaron-courville/

Sam Altman : https://en.wikipedia.org/wiki/Sam_Altman

Sophia : https://en.wikipedia.org/wiki/Sophia_(robot)

www.ingramcontent.com/pod-product-compliance
Lightning Source LLC
Chambersburg PA
CBHW071509220526
45472CB00003B/966